I0137396

DOORWAY TO ECSTASY

A Dancer's Initiation

DOORWAY TO ECSTASY

A Dancer's Initiation

Sherry Brier

Copyright © 2008 Sherry Brier
Revised 2014

ISBN-13: 978-0-9898463-0-1
ISBN-10: 098984630X

All rights reserved. No part of this publication may be reproduced,
stored in a retrieval system, or transmitted in any form or by any
means, electronic, mechanical, recording or otherwise, without the
prior written permission of the author.

Page xi excerpted from Hymn to Hathor from AWAKENING
OSIRIS by Normandi Ellis © 1988 with permission of Phanes Press,
imprint of Red Wheel/Weiser, Newburyport, MA and San Francisco,
CA. www.redwheelweiser.com 1-800-423-7087

Cover photo: *She Brings the Sunset* by Yaniv Golan
Back author's photo: Carl Sermon

Printed in the United States of America

Published by:
Inner Rhythm Productions
518 D Tamalpais Drive
Corte Madera, CA 94925

http://www.InnerRhythmProductions.com
Email: InnerRhythm@comcast.net
Phone: 415-388-6683

DEDICATION

To Richard, my husband and best friend. May we always remember our commitment to meet in the moment and share the beauty of our love with the waiting world.

AUTHOR'S NOTE

Although based on a true story, I call DOORWAY TO ECSTASY a metaphysical memoir, as some of the events transcend ordinary concepts of time and space. The character I call Prema is a composite of all the teachers I've been blessed with along my path. The words she says have come from the mouths of many. The teaching is my synthesis of all I have learned in my many years as both student and teacher.

DOORWAY TO ECSTASY is also a detailed teaching manual of transformational movement and performance. When a new student walks in the door, I immediately see the dancer she can become. I hold that vision in my mind until one day she is inside that image looking out at me. In between, there is much commitment, energy, and hard work for both of us as we follow the paths of initiation outlined in this book. The dancer I'm hoping to reveal is a unique expression of the Spirit. She is an artist who inspires, uplifts, and transports others into the healing world of Beauty.

CONTENTS

"The sun rises or sets now—it matters not.
Here is ecstasy in death and certainty in life.
We are gods in the body of god,
truth and love our destinies.
Go then and make of the world something beautiful,
set up a light in the darkness."
Normandi Ellis

PROLOGUE

Standing in the center of my dance studio, I wait for a new student to arrive. A rather desperate sounding woman had called earlier asking if I would teach private classes for her sixteen-year-old daughter. I wonder what the problem is and how I can be of service.

As the door swings open, a young girl enters yet I find myself looking into the eyes of an old soul. "How can I help you?" I ask, searching her face to see who's behind the purple streaked hair and numerous ear and nose piercings. She twists a lock of hair around her finger with a nervous energy.

"Tell me what you're looking for," I press.

In answer to my question she says quickly but not shyly, "I just got out of three months in the hospital for eating disorders, drug addiction, and suicide attempts. Now I guess I have to learn to love my body instead of abuse it. I always wanted to bellydance and now," she says, her eyes widening, "I have to find ways to get high without the drugs."

"So you've decided to live," I say.

"Yes," she says.

"Then let's begin."

In my thirty years of teaching, I've taught hundreds of students of all ages. They come for all kinds of reasons. Some want the exercise. Many just want to get out of the house one night a week. Others are armchair travelers in motion— exploring different cultures through dance. Some want to learn an art for self-expression, and a small number have dreams of becoming professional dancers. But only a very few come looking for their souls.

I study the girl in front of me as she shifts from foot to foot and fidgets with her rings. This is the kind of student I'm really looking for—one who will pull out of me all that I've learned and ask for who I really am.

As she takes her place behind me, I remember back to when I first met my own teacher. Immersed in a crisis of the heart and spirit, I'd come across some bellydancers in a park. Watching them was the only thing that had given me hope in quite awhile.

Though I am fair-skinned, blonde, and definitely not bare bellybutton material, the movements spoke to me in a long forgotten language. The passion in the music, the abandon of the dancers, and the rapt attention of the audience all drew me. In the midst of swirling veils, clashing cymbals, and booming drums, a door opened, giving me a glimpse of ancient memories and new possibilities. Behind the celebration I sensed the sacred.

Through a seemingly mysterious set of circumstances, I was blessed to find the perfect teacher for me—one who used the dance as a vehicle for healing and conscious development. My mind drifts back to my younger self, to those days when my teacher revealed the secrets and mysteries behind the veil.

INITIATION I:

THE WAY OF TEMPLE DANCE

CHAPTER 1:
KISMET

*T*he veil evokes the faraway untamed places of our imagination," she whispers, gazing off into the distance at something beyond my vision. "Are you willing to explore?" Haunting music drifts from behind the carved wooden screen; the flute and violin weave a spell around each other.

"We've already talked about the veil as wings or as spirit, now what about our nature friends? Can the veil make waves?" Showing me how to follow through with a flick of her wrist, she creates the crest of a breaking wave.

"How about a rainbow?" she asks, wafting the veil from side to side over her head.

"Can you whip up energy like the wind? Like a gentle breeze...an erratic gust...or a tornado?" She progresses from lifting the silk lightly, to flicking it sporadically, to thrashing it furiously around her body. I can hear the fierce wind howling through her veil.

"Now can you evoke the look and feeling of a waterfall...or a fire?" All the while she exaggerates her movements so I can see what she's doing. Her veil conjures up living entities. They morph from one into the other, leaving me spellbound.

Enthralled, I copy her every move. When I capture them correctly, I'm communing directly with nature. I can feel the shift in the atmosphere as the different elements are called into manifestation. Merging with my veil, I'm whirling the Universe into being.

The dream that awakened me faded quickly as I gathered my purse and keys and ran from the house. I was afraid I'd be late for the appointment I'd made the day before. It was my first ray of hope in a dark, difficult and confusing period of my life. I was emotionally and physically at my wits end—depressed, exhausted, and adrift. I thought about the latest turn of events as I drove the road leading out to the East End of Ojai.

A valley in southern California completely surrounded by mountains, Ojai is a place both magical and mystical. The Chumash Indians—the original inhabitants—gave it the name of Ojai, the Nest. Rising above me, the Topa Topa Mountains stood out in high relief against the cloudless sky. They seemed to wait breathlessly for the setting sun to work its splendid magic. Every day as the sun set in the west it turned the striated mountaintop to a glowing color in a spectacle aptly named The Pink Moment.

I'd only recently returned to Ojai, seeking the peace and shelter of the quiet, sleepy valley. I rented a small bungalow just outside of town. Most days found me lying on the bed with my new kitten, Lily Trueheart, sprawled across my chest.

Yesterday morning I felt I just had to get up and go out. I dragged myself to the car and drove up the mountainside toward Matilija Canyon. I hadn't been there for years. The runoff from Matilija Lake trickled like white lace through the massive boulders lining the riverbed. I stopped at the old swimming hole, sat with my back against a gnarled oak tree, and contemplated my predicament.

I was watching the waterfall cascade down the high stone wall into the deep green pool when two women approached. They were speaking intently and didn't notice me as they talked excitedly about Egyptian Temple Dance and a woman named Prema.

Their conversation roused me from my worries about myself. My love of dance and my lifelong fascination with all things Egyptian got the best of me. I jumped up to talk to them. But startled to see me, they quickly walked away, got in their car and left. As they drove off, I felt I'd missed out on an important opportunity, and that threw me into a fit of despair. I drove home sure that I would feel that way forever.

On the way, I stopped to pick up a book at Bart's

Bookstore and as I paid for it, I was drawn to a flyer hanging on the wall behind the counter. A woman named Prema was offering a class called "Egyptian Temple Dance: The Ancient Origin of Bellydance." Thanking my lucky stars for the synchronistic timing, I hurried home and immediately called the contact number. After I answered a few pointed questions, she agreed to see me today for a private class. I could barely sleep last night in anticipation.

Now, driving through the once familiar avocado and orange orchards, I remembered the events that first brought me here. I'd just graduated from college in New England where my boyfriend and I were to marry in three weeks. He was teaching art in a high school in Connecticut and had aspirations of becoming a great painter. We would return from our honeymoon and I also would get a job teaching art and focus on creating my sculptures, which had already gained considerable notice. We would continue working there while plotting to take the New York art world by storm.

A formal wedding was planned, but in a single illuminating moment I had a vision. I saw my whole life laid out in front of me. I saw how it would all unfold, and something in me screamed, "Noooooo…there has to be more!" With tearful regrets I got on a plane the next day, headed off to visit friends in California and never looked back. From the beginning, Ojai was a refuge for me.

It had been several years since I fled from the East Coast and much had happened. I was able to support myself with my art. I lived in beautiful places, drifting back and forth between hip and artsy towns in southern and northern California. But still I was not satisfied. I was searching desperately for something, but I didn't know what.

I was designing and handcrafting jewelry, showing in galleries, and traveling on weekends to art and craft festivals all over the West. The long rides, endless hours spent selling to the public, driving home to make more jewelry, then turning around to do it again the next weekend, had taken it's toll.

My unique mosaic jewelry was beautiful, but my heart wasn't in it anymore. I tried different media. I tried airbrush painting. I tried writing. I tried filmmaking. Changing quickly from one project to another, everything I did was intense and my pace was non-stop. I couldn't find my purpose in life. I couldn't find my proper place in the Universe. Everything seemed so arbitrary. I was looking for more meaning, whatever that meant.

Finally my jangled nerves couldn't handle the fast paced life I'd been living. Awakening one morning with a powerful energy roaring through me, I experienced a heightened sense of alertness, but I was also paralyzed with fear. Then Blair died. A close friend in the prime of his life, he was a new father and a brilliant creative mind. One of life's best promises, you'd think death might have made an exception for him. Wound so tight I thought I might snap, I had so many questions about life and death and what was happening to me. Once again I sought refuge in Ojai.

A cat crossing the road brought me out of my reverie and back to the present. I was speeding down the long straightaway to the far end of the valley. Turning onto Thatcher Road, then left into a dirt driveway, I just missed plowing into a garden filled with long spiny cacti and succulents in every shape imaginable. I'd been distracted by the sight of a blooming century plant. Legend has it that they only flower once every hundred years, and here was one in full blossom—the stalk rising thirty feet into the air. I took it as an auspicious sign.

I parked in front of a small one-story bungalow and walked up the driveway. A Silver Siamese cat with extremely long stilt-like legs walked up the path beside me. The pungent aroma of Indian spices and frying onions wafted out the screen door. Wind chimes hanging above me tinkled in accompaniment to the sounds of chanting coming from within. Before I knocked, a voice inside said, "Come in, I'll be right with you."

Opening the door, I walked into another world. Plants with leaves of every shape and size framed the window, covering one whole wall of the room. The bubbling sound of water from a small fountain created a jungle-like atmosphere in cool contrast to the blazing heat outside. Paintings and sculptures from around the world stood out against the leafy green background. I examined the statuary—a veritable panoply of gods and goddesses—a reclining Buddha, a bronze many-armed Shiva, a dancing goddess, Radha and Krishna with arms entwined. The Egyptian god Horus peaked from behind a large fern while Isis, wings spread, commanded the corner next to the fountain. I was fascinated by the tiny museum filled to the brim with sacred objects.

I felt someone watching me and turned, startled to see the woman from my dream. "The quality of your *attention* is your most important attribute," she said quietly.

I was captivated. Her laser-sharp gaze peered right through me. Henna red curls framed a face with ancient almond shaped eyes, an odd juxtaposition with her pale slightly freckled skin. Dressed in full flowing black pants and a fitted black top, the only color came from her flaming red hair and mysterious green eyes. Long gold earrings peaked from behind her wedge shaped haircut with its Cleopatra style bangs. She was ageless.

"And the *intention* that you set before yourself will guide and create your life. But first you must see yourself clearly and discover who you really are. This dance will teach you to focus your attention so you'll have the will and energy to fill your life with your own intention."

"Come," she said, "we'll talk later."

I stood facing her in the place she indicated. She raised both arms out to her sides, and as she inhaled they seemed to float up above her. When she exhaled they fanned down, changing the atmosphere in the room. It got lighter, as if someone had opened the blinds, and more quiet…

"Follow me," she said. "I will tell you what we are doing as we go along."

I raised and lowered my arms with her. "The whole class is a ritual from beginning to end," she began. "What people in this country call bellydance is, in essence, a solo improvisational dance for women. Most of the rest of the world call it Oriental dance, which translates as 'the dance from the East.' Women have danced this way since the time of Eve."

Continuing the movement, she went on, "From well before the age of the pharaohs, priestesses in ancient Egypt executed these slow movements. If I accept you as a student, you will study with me as a modern day priestess-in-training, to become an intermediary between Heaven and Earth. You'll learn to empty yourself to be receptive to higher energies and also strengthen your body to withstand the powerful frequencies that wish to manifest through it. This ritual will help you do both." She stopped for a moment to make sure she had my attention.

"This is ancient and hidden knowledge, veiled in secrecy. It's serious business and not to be taken lightly. You must have an unwavering commitment, as all gifts from behind the veil must be earned by a strong will and hard work." She looked sternly at me as if measuring my mettle.

"Feel your feet on the floor," she instructed. "Imagine that they have roots growing down to the center of the Earth, anchoring you to the planet. Bring your awareness up to your center—the space inside in the middle of your body, slightly below your navel. Now lift through the ribs."

We continued circling our arms out to the side, up overhead, then back down again. "Allow your knees to bend as you push your energy into the Earth and say to yourself, 'I am grounded in my feet.' Bring your attention up to your midsection and affirm, 'I am centered in my belly.' And as you pull your ribs up say, 'I am lifted in my heart.'" Immediately, I felt lighter. "This is where you must always begin," she said. "You cannot learn anything if you aren't totally here, present, grounded in the moment."

Taking a handful of hair from the top of my head and pulling it straight up, she said, "Imagine a line that goes from the Sun above, through your head, down the length of your body, and then connects with the center of the Earth. This is your vertical axis. This alignment will allow you to be in an upright and ready position for dancing. It will also allow the life energy to run up and down your body unimpeded by knots in your spine. With a straight spine you can become a direct connection between the Sun and the Earth."

We continued these movements as she urged me to become aware of my breath. "Exhale on the downward and inward movements and inhale on the up and out movements. Think of your body as a balloon. You want to fill it with air so it rises effortlessly. Then you exhale to let the air out and bring it back to Earth."

This class was not what I'd imagined while driving out to the East End. I had visions of the dancers I'd seen recently at a festival in the park, and I wanted to dance with the same passion and abandon they expressed. I'd hoped this class would distract me from my preoccupation with my problems. I was startled when, as if she could hear my inner musings, Prema said, "You know, you can't run away."

I wondered what I had gotten myself into. Who was this person? And what was really hidden behind the veil? How would this help me get back to normal? So many questions, but Prema just kept moving.

Coming to a close she raised her arms overhead, then with palms together, she drew them down to rest over her midsection. She nodded her head, looked into my eyes and said, "Thank you." She gestured to two chairs in the corner by the fountain, "Sit while I get us a cool drink. It's best to let the energy settle before we speak."

When she returned with tall glasses of iced tea, the burning questions I had come with seemed not so important, at least not pressing enough to break this peaceful moment. "Yes," she nodded as if she heard my thoughts, "we often find the answer to our questions in the stillness following this work."

✳ ✳ ✳

Prema hadn't set a time for another class, so I wasn't sure when I called if she would allow me to return. I was surprised at how relieved I was when she told me to come next week at the same time. In between, I thought about the first class yet didn't really know what to make of it. I imagined it as some sort of interview. This time I was really longing to learn some steps; I was ready to start dancing.

I arrived early, wanting to talk with Prema about my fears and anxiety and the physical symptoms they were creating. The first time I'd come I hadn't wanted to divulge my problems, fearing that she wouldn't want to teach someone with a lot of baggage. The vibrations in my chest were so constant and strong, that I'd finally gone to a doctor to make sure I wasn't having a heart attack. Reassuring me that there was nothing wrong with my heart, he said I should learn to relax and that exercise would do me good. Then he offered to give me a prescription for some pills, which I refused.

When Prema answered the door she was wiping the paint from a large artist's brush. Placing it on an easel in a corner of the studio, below a canvas splattered with brilliant colors, she motioned me to the same space as last time. When I began telling her about my troubles, she interrupted me to say that she had accepted me as a student, not in spite of, but because of these symptoms. She said I should trust that she knew how to address them. Surprised and embarrassed that I was not hiding my problems very well, I asked her how she knew. She said only, "I know about these things," then told me to stand behind her so we could begin.

I took my place. We repeated the same sequence of movements and then Prema said, "Let's find our posture for the dance. If you are in the proper posture you will be able to do the steps correctly. Your posture in dance is the most important technique you will learn and also the most difficult thing to maintain. Your posture is to your body…as your attitude is to your mind."

She saw me fidgeting, wanting to get on with the dancing part, and repeated, "Your posture is to your body…as your attitude is to your mind. This is a very important and deep concept," she said sharply. "Dance is a metaphor for life. Just as life is a constant challenge to maintain the proper attitude, the continual struggle for the whole career of a dancer is learning to maintain the proper posture.

"Feel your feet on the Earth," she commanded. "Extend your energy down into it. Unlock your knees." She tapped the back of my hyper-extended knees until they softened. "They must have a give to them, like shock absorbers they must cushion your movements. Drop your tailbone."

Like a little Napoleon, she continued barking out orders. "Now bring the rib cage forward and pull your belly muscles up. Not tight, but up…the ribs balanced both front and back. Shoulders down, back of neck long, head perched lightly on the neck, eyes up and looking out." I felt like I was being strapped into a straight jacket.

"Everyone stands with their rear ends sticking out. This is why most of the adult population have back problems. Our spines are meant to be straight, so the energy can run up and down freely and the muscles can strengthen and support the vertebrae correctly."

"Now breathe," she said as she touched my puffed up chest. I popped like a balloon and exhaled loudly.

"You mean I have to breathe too?" I laughed. But I did feel completely different.

"Your posture is to your body…as your attitude is to your mind," she repeated emphatically. "Look," she said, as she assumed a powerful dynamic stance. "This way you're saying, 'I am here. I am ready. I would like to dance for you. I am vigilant. I stand guard at the temple. I'm a warrior. I am a priestess." She paused then dropped her chest back and pushed her hands away from her body. "This posture says, 'I don't want to be here. Don't look at me. I have nothing to give.'"

We spent the rest of the class slackening our muscles and drooping, then pulling up to a grounded-centered-balanced posture. Over and over we went from rag doll to poised dancer. Though my muscles felt slightly tired, the energy rushing through my body actually felt good. Like a finely tuned car, it purred.

As I drove home, Prema's words, mentioned so casually, reverberated in my ears. "Dance is a metaphor for life!"

The phrase kept running through my mind in an endless loop. I could barely contain myself, hoping it might be the solution to my current dilemma—one I'd had throughout my life. I always thought that whoever was in charge had just forgotten to give me the manual that ought to come with having a human body. It seemed like someone should know what was really going on.

Even as a child, I felt there was some secret they weren't telling me. Others seemed to go easily about life in very untroubled, uninspired, and uncreative ways. They just didn't have the questions I did. I was always asking, what does it mean? Is it this way or that way? Why? Why not?

"Dance is a metaphor for life…life is a dance." If I could follow this trail of reasoning, perhaps I'd finally get some answers to my burning questions—what should I do with my life, why are we here, what's it all about? I felt like I was on the verge of a great discovery. With this small taste I felt some hope; my sense of relief was overwhelming. Maybe I was on the right track after all. I couldn't wait to see Prema again.

Parking at the foot of the driveway, I climbed out of the car and assumed the proper posture. Walking slowly, I tried to maintain my poise. I felt Prema's eyes on me, watching through the kitchen window.

We began once again with the same movements, more quickly this time and without speaking. I was beginning to feel more relaxed. Between classes I'd spent a lot of time finding the two-way stretch pulling me from my center. Simultaneously, I felt like a tree reaching for the Sun above and for the water deep inside the Earth.

Experiencing myself as so pliable really changed my walking. I felt like those naturally graceful women in third world countries who seem so comfortable with their bodies and glide so effortlessly with baskets on their heads. On my rare forays into town to send my jewelry off to the galleries, I noticed people watching me.

I could feel when I was, or wasn't, balanced around my central axis and even remembered to breathe sometimes. Though I still felt like I was about to tip over when I found the correct posture, I did feel more alert, ready, and primed to respond like a runner at the starting line.

"Only now are you prepared to begin with some of the movements of the dance," Prema began. "Before, you would have hurt your back doing these isolation movements, because your muscles would have been straining in the wrong direction. Many dancers have back problems because they dance with their tushes in outer space.

"I, on the other hand," she flipped her palm over, "have overcome the effect of severe scoliosis by doing this dance in the proper posture. Doctors told me thirty years ago that I would spend my life in a wheelchair. But baby," she struck a cheesecake pose, "look at me now." I didn't know whether to laugh or not, she'd been so serious up until then.

I wanted to ask about her past, and for that matter, her present and her future. I was fascinated with everything about Prema, but out of respect I hadn't questioned her. I sensed that our relationship wasn't personal, and I was afraid my curiosity might put it in jeopardy. Luckily, she continued on before I opened my mouth.

"We begin with hip circles. This is a dance of isolations, one part of the body moves as the other part creates a stable structure." Her hips moved in tiny tight circles.

"Remember again, dance is a metaphor for life. Everything I say about the dance and your movements is directly applicable to your life."

She saw me searching for the connection in my mind.

"In this instance, to do these hip movements correctly, you must gather yourself around your center and lock your rib cage in place. This creates a strong structure in your upper body, so you can freely move your lower body without losing your balance." She paused for a moment to make sure I got it. "You could meditate on this one instruction for a lifetime. You want to learn to ground yourself in one area of your life. Then you can let your spirit soar without being open to negative forces."

The hip circles were pleasurable. But just as I started losing myself in the repetitive movements, Prema clapped her hands loudly. "Stay awake!" she commanded. Startled, I almost fell over.

"Stay awake," she repeated. "The purpose of the dance is to become more aware on many levels, not to fall asleep. Concentrate on the center of the circle. Feel that point. That is your first chakra."

I was somewhat familiar with the word, but I thought it was an East Indian term. I looked at her expectantly.

"Chakra is a *Sanskrit* word from India for the many energy centers located throughout your body. We will find, awaken, and generate energy in the seven major chakras." She indicated that I should keep moving as she spoke.

"All ancient evolved cultures show knowledge of the chakra system in their art. The Egyptian's written history on this subject was lost, probably in the fiery destruction of the Alexandria library. But this knowledge is even reflected in the placement of the temples along the Nile. Each temple is dedicated to a god or goddess who represented the qualities governed by a particular chakra in the human body.

"These ritual movements I'll be teaching you originated in ancient Egypt. They are the predecessors of yoga and tai chi and the basis of the meridian system in acupuncture. Let's remember our purpose here," she looked deeply into my eyes. "The temple priestesses used these exercises to prepare their bodies to receive higher energies, so they would have the wisdom and intuition to guide and heal their people. Our intention is to bring awareness to the energy center, or chakra, we are moving around. Attention and breath and movement are the healers."

She looked pointedly at me, "What did I just say?" she asked.

I was a little annoyed because I *had* been listening. "Attention and breath and movement are the healers," I repeated.

"Good," she nodded, "it's so easy to overlook the most important pearls of wisdom when they sound so simple."

Class was over, but I was reluctant to leave. Looking around the studio, which in a typical house would be the living room, I was enchanted by the colors and textures of all the exotic objects. The long stretch of mirrors doubled the empty space in the center and reflected the wonderful treasures lining the walls and hanging from the ceiling.

The first time I came I'd briefly examined the mini jungle of plants surrounding the window. With the fountain, sculptures, and high backed rattan chairs, this area was so enveloping that I felt like I was inside a greenhouse. The other side of the room held the easel and several paintings stacked facing the wall. Next to the canvases sat a worktable with paints and other art supplies arranged in an orderly manner. In the corner closer to the mirror stood a large four-panel, carved Indian screen that Prema periodically disappeared behind to change the music. Embroidered textiles and intricately patterned saris draped casually over its top and sides.

Opposite the mirror, two doorways strung with beads tinkled or clattered when Prema entered the rooms beyond. Egyptian drums of different sizes and shapes, made from engraved metal or glazed clay, hugged the perimeter. Other musical instruments, along with swords, canes, masks, headdresses, and a variety of costume parts climbed up the walls.

Not even the ceiling escaped decoration. A fan with palm frond-like blades turned lazily, creating a breeze that brought an eight-foot hanging Chinese paper dragon to life. In the corners hung antique Moroccan lamps. Light peeked through shapes cut from the hammered brass and illuminated the red, blue, green, and amber stained glass panels.

Whether it was the atmosphere, the movements, or Prema herself, this was the only place I felt hopeful and not at the mercy of my confusion. I believed my questions were going to be answered, and that somehow my path led right through this room. I lingered but as I got my things together, Prema was already picking up her paintbrush.

"Practice," she said as I carefully closed the screen door.

I laughed on my way home. What was I going to practice, one hip circle? One hip circle does not a dancer make. I wasn't learning what I had expected, and I sure wasn't dancing...but something kept drawing me back there.

At home I added the hip circle to the other movements. I practiced because I thought Prema would know if I hadn't. Otherwise, I feared she might send me away for lack of commitment.

When I arrived for class, I found Prema sitting on the ground in the cactus garden. Bending over a group of newly planted baby cacti, she looked like Mother Nature herself. I'm sure I heard her murmuring to the plants before rising and leading me into the studio.

After our opening ritual we began again with hip circles. I focused, and soon the circles were smooth and effortless. "Find the center point of that circle and breathe into it," Prema instructed. "Now exhale and radiate your energy." I wasn't sure what she meant.

"Imagine you are standing in the center of the Universe. Lines extend from *your* center in infinite directions. Consciously send your breath and your energy out along these lines. Ultimately you will use them as lines of communication, like a telephone line. They will connect you to everything. You'll be able to gather and send whatever is necessary at any moment from anywhere in the cosmos."

I was excited; I'd never heard such a thing before. Immediately closing my eyes, I inhaled and exhaled repeatedly waiting for something to happen. "Nothing's happening," I said with frustration.

Prema just laughed at my impatience. "Eventually you will be able to do this with just a thought. For now, the movements will help you find and focus your energy and awareness on your center or on a particular chakra. This is why moving meditation is much better for Western people."

I asked Prema to explain.

"I taught yoga for many years," she answered, "but found that it's often not as accessible. Of course, in yoga you are using your body, but you hold static poses and sometimes static poses lead to inflexible minds. The Temple Dance I am teaching you is the quickest way to move beyond the mind that imprisons us in ordinary reality. The rhythmic flow of the movement, along with the ritual figures and postures, changes our somatic perception. This combination alters our consciousness and allows us to experience different realities and eventually ecstatic states of being.

"Our minds are usually so busy that sitting meditation—trying to use the mind to quiet the mind, or being still and watching the breath—is difficult for Westerners. The body fidgets like an unruly pet. It's good to give the body something to do.

"Also," she added, "your body has it's own wisdom embedded in its genetic code. Why not let it help you? Don't see your body as the enemy or try to restrict it like a naughty child. Instead, guide it and let it reveal its knowledge to you."

These were refreshing ideas for me. After always hearing that you have to reject or subjugate the body to reach higher states of awareness, Prema's approach seemed actually do-able.

"Now, let your attention move between the center of the circle and the circle you are drawing in space," she brought me back from my ruminations and reminded me to continue the movements while listening to her. "We will talk about all this another time. Better to just feel than to understand sometimes, no?"

For someone like me, who held on for dear life to my rational mind, letting go and just feeling was actually terrifying. I felt I was drifting off into space without a lifeline. I began to shake.

Aware of my plight, Prema said calmly, "Bring your attention back to your body…let it guide you into the moment…it's a doorway to ecstasy."

"What do you mean?" I asked with urgency. Her words had hit me like a thunderbolt.

"The literal meaning of ecstasy is 'to stand outside the body.' Use your body as a doorway, an entrance, a starting point to go beyond the ordinary experience of reality, beyond rational thought. Focusing and attending to your body will bring you back from the limited places you repeatedly inhabit in your mind."

The tone of Prema's voice changed; she sounded as if she was calling to me from afar. "Come…come back into your body…step through the doorway into an infinitely vast world…that world is here…that world is now…ecstasy is what *now* feels like…ecstasy is the natural bliss of being…right here, right now."

Feeling a jolt as if I'd just landed on a runway, my eyes were riveted on Prema's face. A look of pure joy settled across her features. "The dancing body is sublime," she sighed, as her eyes got brighter. "And dancing to inspired music…ahhhh…she closed her eyes taking in the experience. For a moment I felt like I was intruding on her private moment, but then I swear I could hear divine music pulling me in to share her otherworldly rapture.

Prema's energy was so strong that I took off with her. I soared into the heart of Now. The sense of freedom and wide-open space was beyond anything I had ever imagined. It may have lasted a moment or a lifetime. It was enough to know I had to learn the way to find this magical feeling for myself. I had to learn to get there on my own. We returned together and looked into each other's eyes. It was too intense; I had to look away.

I spent the time between sessions with Prema considering my body as never before. Suddenly I would become aware of my feet or my hands, the wonder of them and how they worked. I was amazed that I even had a body at all. Where did it come from? How miraculous! Recalling Prema's words, it seemed a great paradox that the body was both a doorway to the real world and also something that had to be tamed like a rambunctious pet.

When I'd confided my physical and emotional distress to Prema, she explained that if I didn't resist the force moving through my body, but instead made friends with it, I would be more comfortable and less afraid. Trying to let go while doing my practices did seem to allow the energy to move around more freely, but still, I was often paralyzed with fear.

I also worked on radiating. Though Prema had talked about this being the tool used to project healing energy, it appealed to my adventurous nature that yearned to be everywhere and see everything. The thought that I could be here in my living room, but experience far off exotic places, drove me to practice more.

When I wasn't trying to escape into a world of glamour and excitement, I became aware of another more mystical reality existing right beyond the everyday one. It called to me in a whisper. I sometimes caught a momentary glimpse when a breeze wafted the veil aside, revealing an elusive image that quickly faded into the insistence of ordinary life.

CHAPTER 2:
UNCHARTED TERRITORY

W hen I arrived for my private class, Prema let me in then quickly closed both doors to keep the hot air out. It was over a hundred sweltering degrees outside. Mercifully, the ceiling fan created a bit of coolness in the otherwise stifling afternoon heat. Finishing our opening ritual, we began with hip circles. "Continue moving," Prema instructed, "while I tell you some things.

"As your practice unfolds, you will learn to split your attention in several directions at the same time. This will allow you to become more and more aware on many levels. Most people can barely stay focused on one thing at a time. No wonder they say we use only five percent of our brain. People are so sure they know what's happening, so quick to rule out anything they can't see with their own eyes or comprehend with their puny five percent."

She stopped talking to check out my movements. "Be aware of the circle you're making," she reminded, "and also keep your attention on its center." I continued moving, shifting my awareness between the center of the circle and the circle my hips were drawing. I felt a warmth and a tingling begin around my coccyx.

"Very good," Prema nodded, acknowledging my experience. I was mystified by how she immediately knew whenever my awareness changed.

"Because of this force running through your body, which you do not yet see as a gift, you have a sensitivity that allows you to feel things that most people are never aware of. Most people live unaware that they are actually energy bodies and are afraid when they feel any rush in the body at all. Temple dancing will allow you to gain control of this virtually unlimited fount of energy and use it for a world that is in dire need of healing."

She gave me a moment to let her words sink in. "It is so naïve for people to believe the origin of bellydance is merely a child birthing ritual, and that it's only use now is for entertainment."

Shaking her head and sighing deeply, she gazed out the window for several moments. Then, as if returning from afar, she picked up where she left off. "It's not their fault. Because they don't have an alternate way to look at things, people hold tight to the ordinary and try to define life using concepts that jibe with the status quo. They are afraid to step outside the known and contemplate other possibilities. Even though they're unhappy and bored to death, they are more comfortable with the consensus view of reality."

Prema took a deep breath followed by a long exhale. "The world is so big, so miraculous, but people fight to the death to maintain a very limited concept of life. In their need to feel safe and comfortable, they accept a false sense of security. In their endless desire for power over others, they're willing to perpetuate a notion of reality that causes sickness, war, and strife."

Her voice became more insistent, "We need new inspiration, a new vision, a broader paradigm of possibility." Again she turned toward the light filtering through the window, her eyes opening wider as if trying to unlock the shuttered vision of humanity. She seemed to suffer a profound sorrow, then shaking it off, she continued.

"So, back to the origin and purpose of bellydance. All the other developed ancient cultures had their dances and rituals for bringing in the higher spirits and energy. Why would Egypt, the grandest of them all, be any different? Just look at their symbols and it becomes evident what this dance is about."

I was busily trying to stay aware of my outer circle, my center point, and not miss a word of what Prema was saying. "Please tell me more," I urged.

She seemed to be considering if I was really up to focusing on so many things at once. She decided to give it a try. "You asked the other day about the function of this first chakra you are drawing circles around." I nodded. "Have you ever seen the symbol of the American Medical Association?" she asked.

I thought I must have missed a beat.

"It is the same symbol associated with Thoth, the Egyptian god of healing, medicine, and wisdom. It is a picture of two snakes wrapped around a central wand or staff. They join at the top in a pair of wings. The snakes represent the positive and negative energy poles winding their way up the central axis of the body. They move up from the physical world at the base of the spine and join with the spiritual, symbolized by the wings."

"But what does that have to do with bellydance?" I was concentrating as hard as I could, but I thought I had missed something.

"This symbol has surfaced in many cultures and been attributed to many mythical figures. It is a sign of the Greek god Hermes and the Roman god Mercury, and it's also carved at the entrance to Hindu temples. What did these different cultures have in common?"

I didn't have a clue. I waited as she observed my hip circles.

"Their mythology and religions evolved from the even more ancient goddess religions. As we see in the sculpture and painting from pre-written history, the Goddess was the acknowledged creator of the world. In Egypt she was called Ua Zit. She was personified by the symbol of the cobra. The word goddess in hieroglyphics is the same as the word for cobra. Even now, a word in English for priestess or prophetess is pythoness, which means a woman possessed by the spirit of an oracle.

"An oracle is somebody or something considered to be a source of knowledge, wisdom, or prophecy. Isis and Matt, the two supreme goddesses of Egyptian mythology, wore the cobra crown. The bellydance is a dance of the muscles. It emulates the movements of the snake that sheds its outer skin and is a symbol of transformation. The dances of many different cultures evolved from the visual depictions of their creation mythologies and the rituals they used to summon the Goddess."

Told in the context of my practice, I was fascinated by the information Prema was sharing with me. Normally I wasn't interested in mythological stories or poetry either. I was usually so busy speeding along to get the plot, that I wanted my reading to cut to the chase.

"People have been arguing the origins and meanings of religion and symbols forever. It doesn't really matter if you believe in the interpretation of different rituals or agree upon their origin. The important thing is to practice them and to realize the potential this dance has for transformation right now."

Glancing again at my hip circles, Prema nodded and went on. "So back to the function of the first chakra. This base or root chakra governs our sense of survival, whether we feel we have a foundation and support. The state of this chakra determines if we feel safe and secure in our bodies, and whether we trust that we will have our basic needs met. People who are balanced in this chakra feel alive and grounded and trust that they are able to take care of themselves. Those who are imbalanced in this chakra have fears of death, lack confidence, and may be greedy or jealous for fear that they won't have enough.

"As you focus your attention with these hip circles, you'll become aware of the state of energy in your first chakra. Your reaction to the movements becomes a barometer of your emotional life. Your thoughts and feelings will tell you what you need to know.

"At times you might think that this work is causing or increasing the discomfort and distress you may feel. But it is actually bringing your attention to what is already locked into that area. Attention, breath, and movement are the tools that will heal the imbalance. Your attention and breath will channel the healing energy to that area, and the repetitive circles will create a balanced pattern out of the chaos that has accumulated from various experiences. You have to be willing to go through the unpleasantness to get to the other side."

As I gathered my things to leave, Prema held the door open for me. "I would be willing to bet that a lot of the problems you're having right now have to do with your first chakra."

I was aware that our past experiences could be accessed through hypnosis. The idea that memories are stored in particular parts of the body, and that each part governs certain energies, sounded promising. I was so hopeful, that it was no problem making myself practice. I soon found though, that it was no walk in the park.

As I worked with the first chakra, a pattern of fears beginning in my childhood, resurfaced to haunt me. Mostly they had lurked in the background creating a constant subtle agitation. Now they became full blown. I never walked into a building without checking for the exits in case of an earthquake. I developed a fear of flying so debilitating that I wouldn't get on a plane. Even on the ground, I didn't feel safe. I was absolutely sure some plane flying overhead might fall out of the sky and hit me.

I began to question if this work was really for me. After all, I just wanted to learn to dance and get rid of this excess energy that was getting in the way of my life. It seemed my problems were getting more intense. I longed to get back to normal. Instead, I was beginning a journey down an unknown road that was taking me further away.

Hoping that I could talk to Prema about my fears and reservations, I got to class early. "Take all that energy and put it into the movements," Prema interrupted as I started to blurt out my concerns. "Learn to bring everything to the dance. Bring your fears, your turmoil, and the good things too—your hopes, your love. Bring it all to the dance and eventually it will be like coming home." As we flowed quietly through the ritual, my mind calmed and the tension left my body.

"Today we'll add hip figure eights," Prema's hips were already in motion, showing me the figure I was to make. "These are movements around the second chakra. There are four different figure eights. Actually, they are lying down, so think of them as infinity signs." She showed me how to make the shape in both forward and backward directions and to keep the eights parallel to the floor.

"Now that you see the outward eight, feel the tiny eight you are making around your central axis. Know that these movements are all internal, growing out of your center. As you move, think *center-out-center-out.* " Concentrating on the inside eight, I felt a warmth and a tingling begin in my genital area. It was both soothing and exciting.

"Don't worry," Prema said. "This chakra governs both your emotions and your sexual energy. You must come alive in this center. Your sexual energy is the source, on the physical level, of what will become spiritual energy. Many people seeking to become more spiritual want to deny their sexuality. They've been conditioned to think it's a lower or grosser energy. But as you continue with your practices, you will learn to transform and refine it."

As we continued moving, Prema explained, "The second chakra is also the storage center of the emotions. All past experiences are stored somewhere in the body. As you work with these movements you will probably bring up memories long forgotten. When you open these centers, you'll find all kinds of recollections coming to the surface. That is why it is so important to be grounded and centered.

"This work will become a mirror for you to observe yourself. The way you come to your practice every morning will show you who you are and what you're made of. It will strip your veils of illusion away and expose you in a way a regular mirror never could. You will come to know yourself and who your gods are—whom you are worshiping with your actions and thoughts. The ancient Egyptians' first and most important commandment was 'Know thyself...and thou shalt know the Universe and God'.

"I've seen so many students come to the dance and then run off when all the memories they've suppressed start coming up. Just when they're really getting somewhere," she shrugged. "They're afraid to deal with uncomfortable feelings. Sherry, you shouldn't let the power of these painful emotions stop you. You *can* move through them."

I stopped moving for a moment.

"Any questions?" she asked.

"You've given me so much information, how am I going to remember it all?" I wondered aloud.

"I give you this information to create a context for your practice, to pique your interest on more levels, to give you motivation to continue when it gets difficult or uncomfortable. The important thing is just to practice," she said emphatically.

Bringing me back once again to my body, Prema showed me the down eights and up eights. "While the previous two figure eights were drawn parallel to the floor," she explained, "we trace these two in a vertical plane." Drawing an infinity sign on the mirror, she illustrated how we could make the direction of these movements begin either up or down.

We ended by going over the figure eights in four directions, then Prema asked, "What's the important thing?"

"Just practice," I answered.

At home I worked with the second chakra movements. Not only did I feel my own emotions arising, but I began intensely experiencing other people's feelings. It was as if I was privy to their inner lives. Then I started to remember my repressed childhood and some devastating incidences that I'd completely forgotten.

Prema had urged me to create a witness—a part of myself that could stand back and observe rather than react. This was not an easy job. I kept getting immediately swept up in my feelings. My emotions were strongly polarized. Love, hate. Peace, fear. Happy, sad. I vacillated back and forth between these opposite states as if swinging from a chandelier. My anger registered off the charts, and I seemed to fly off the handle at the slightest provocation.

In my quieter times, I worked with the ritual and particularly with the figure eights, trying to watch myself from the outside. I remembered that as a child, I wanted to be a rock star. I'd sing along with the radio at the top of my lungs, imagining the whole world watching and adoring me.

Now, bit-by-bit, I began to develop a witness. I moved back and forth between being totally in my body and feeling the movements, then switching to watch myself from the outside. I practiced being my own audience. More and more, in the heat of an emotional moment, I would remember to become the witness rather than the actor immersed in those heavy emotions.

Going about my days, I watched myself as if I was a character in a play and wondered what I had done all the years when I didn't have this concept of a witness. Observing myself in this way created just enough distance to get centered before I reacted. It became clear to me that one of my biggest coping mechanisms was overeating. To stuff down my feelings, I was self-medicating with food.

I also found myself indulging in erotic fantasies. I felt like a young girl at puberty, seeing everyone as a sexual being and wondering about his or her private life. This created problems I didn't need. I was attracting a lot of unwanted attention from all kinds of men, even though I was sure I wasn't acting differently.

Dealing with these emotional side effects was very hard work, and I often felt like giving up. I originally thought I was taking dance lessons to get away from my problems and maybe even to enjoy myself. Instead, I was face to face with a whole lifetime of unresolved emotions and memories. Some days I just wanted to run screaming from the house, but something inside kept drawing me back to my practice.

∗ ∗ ∗

Walking quickly up Prema's driveway with my witness at my side, I felt like I had an invisible friend. Before the door even closed behind me, I was telling Prema about my struggles, and that I was amazed that I actually kept practicing despite how little will I usually had. "This is really good," she responded. "You are creating a magnetic center, something inside that is stronger than your usual tendencies. It's a will toward the light. You are developing a part of yourself that wants to overcome your weaknesses and emerge from the shadows. It is an ally, and it will only get stronger with continued practice."

She stepped back and seemed to observe me closely, then nodded her head up and down. "This is good," she repeated. "Come, let us continue our practice."

"This is the time to become aware of where the movements originate in your body. Whether you are walking, making steps, doing isolations, or shimmying, all the movements, from the waist down, begin from the gluteus muscles. As I told you the other day, this is why some people call bellydance a snake dance. Done properly, it all comes from the muscles expanding and contracting. This creates that serpent-like quality.

"All your upper body and arm movements come from the big back muscles surrounding your shoulder blades. As in life, everything comes from the invisible world behind you, into the visible world. Remember," she stopped moving to emphasize her point, "energy comes through you…is transformed by your intention…and then moves out into the world."

I was beginning to see how vast and complex this study would be.

Again, as if she knew my thoughts, Prema said, "Things can be as simple or complex as you make them. These ideas are simple when we *do* and *experience* them, but get very abstract when we try to talk about them. It is important, though, to be conscious on a verbal level of what we are learning. But always remember, *the word is not the thing.* "

This got my attention big time. Such a simple phrase, but I had never heard it before. It was liberating in the moment, but the more I thought about it the shakier my already fragile world became. If all the ideas and explanations about life were not real, then what was? What could I hang onto?

Prema was quietly watching me go through my mental machinations. Like a drowning puppy, I looked at her for help. She said only one thing, "There is nowhere to fall."

The realizations of the last class kept me very busy. I found myself examining everything. I looked at things as if I'd never seen them before. I wouldn't name them right away but kept looking as if I didn't know what they were. Whether I was seeing people or objects, the longer I looked the more alive and interesting they became.

I felt like an alien who had just arrived on Earth. Everything was new to me. I was riveted to whatever I observed, taking it all in. Every time I said something, I felt the gap between the words I was using and the thing itself. I experienced how I thought I knew my whole world because I could name it. But when I didn't label it, everything was unfamiliar, fascinating, and exquisitely beautiful. *The word is not the thing* became my mantra.

I came to class with great anticipation. Working with the exercises, I began to feel a bit of control over the process that seemed to be ravaging my body. Prema explained that when I did learn to control the energy, I would be grateful it had chosen to visit me. She reminded me that most people never have the satisfaction of finding their true purpose in life. She assured me that when I entered the ecstatic states of higher consciousness, I would never be sorry about going through this difficult and painful transformation. She said it was a blessing and should be invited. I, on the other hand, experienced it as an interloper that was ruining my life.

I did find that while working with these movements, I could bring all the excess energy down to the first and second chakras. I felt I had it trapped. Like a caged tiger, it paced back and forth in my lower torso. Confined in that one area, it was still threatening, but I could keep a watchful eye on it.

I was amazed at how potent these methods were and wondered again why I had never heard about the power of bellydance. I asked Prema, "Do the Egyptian dancers have this knowledge you're teaching me about their dance?"

"Even right there at the source, it's difficult to find teachers who are aware of the esoteric traditions," she answered. "Children learn the dance as a social activity at the sides of their mothers and female relatives. Because it's so ingrained as an entertainment, people often don't look back on its history. And they often don't see its spiritual roots, especially in cultures in the Middle East that have such a love-hate relationship with the dance."

"What do you mean?"

"They love and adore their favorite dancers and make them stars, but they have so many cultural prejudices about how women should behave.

"You mean in the Koran?"

"No, actually the Koran doesn't have all these gender related laws. As usual, it's a small minority of religious leaders who want power over people, so they impose laws and attribute them to the scriptures. They seem to be conflicted about their own sexuality, so they transfer blame for their desires onto women, and especially dancers. On the one hand they love them, while on the other they think of them as whores.

"The dancers are a part of every celebration from weddings to circumcisions, but family members would die if their daughter wanted to be a dancer or their son wanted to marry one. So the dance tradition is looked upon with varying degrees of disdain.

"Even now, in some Middle Eastern countries there are morality police watching to see if women are observing the laws attributed to the Koran. There is still a civil law about dancers covering their midsections, though the dancers wear very sheer body stockings to comply and still have the look they want in costumes. Periodically, the religious fundamentalists threaten the dancers, who are forced to move to other countries to continue their careers."

Everything about the dance fascinated me—the history, both past and present, the practices, the costumes, and the benefits I felt so immediately. I was entering an ancient esoteric tradition and was very grateful to be involved in something so rich and so untapped in the West.

Arriving for my lesson, I found Prema in the act of creation. Never failing to amaze me with her versatility, she sat on a chair in the garden with a tray balanced on her lap. Tiny glass beads of every color and shade sparkled as she picked them up with a long thin needle and added them to the intricate pattern already in process.

"A necklace," she said offhandedly as she rose. I wanted to admire it, but Prema placed the tray on her chair and led me inside.

"Today we move our attention up to the third chakra located in the solar plexus area." Prema showed me how to draw circles with my ribs. "Push from the back muscles, set the movement in motion, then relax and let it continue around. The energy of the moves are *yang*, which means to make an effort," she pushed the center of my back, "then *yin*, which means to relax and let it unfold effortlessly."

"Aren't these Chinese principles?" I asked while continuing the movements.

"Yes, but they are the best way to describe what I want to talk about, so why not use them?"

"Aren't yin and yang forces of darkness and light?" I questioned.

"Yes, but they also refer to all sets of opposing forces. And the reality is that they don't exist alone, there is always some yang in the yin and vise versa. On our path, the idea that's important is that they are in balance, and balance is a concept that we easily understand with our bodies.

"That's why the way of dance is such an accessible spiritual path—we all have bodies and we all can move. We are able to feel the laws of the Universe played out right here in the laboratory of our bodies. All the profound truths become immediately obvious through our dance experience. Finding a balance between yin and yang will benefit us in every area of our lives, especially in the realms governed by the third chakra."

Prema placed the palm of her hand above my bellybutton. "This chakra is where personal power is stored. When you say 'I will,' this is where it comes from." She repeated, "I will," in a strong resounding voice. Listening to her, I really believed that anything she said after that would be accomplished.

"If you have a weak *I* and can't seem to make anything happen, this is the area to work on. Your movements should be an extension of your breath. Like riding waves—inhale and make an effort to move up the wave, then exhale and coast down the other side.

"Try it," she nodded to me. "Connect the rib circles to your breath." I began breathing as I thought she wanted. "Don't breathe so heavily or you'll hyperventilate and pass out," Prema laughed, reaching out to steady me.

"You mean that if I make these rib circles around my third chakra I'll be able to complete my unfinished projects?" As a perpetual procrastinator, I jumped at the idea of developing my will. Especially now. Though I was too sensitive to go out amongst throngs of people and sell at the art shows, I still had to make my jewelry to support myself. The gallery owners were calling me, alarmed that they hadn't received their orders. But the constant vibrations in my chest and the anxiety they created made it almost impossible for me to concentrate.

"Manifesting is not quite that easy," Prema answered. "One of the most difficult things in the world is learning to *do*." Noting my disappointment, she added, "But it does help if you know the secrets of manifesting."

"Do you know the secrets? Will you tell me?"

When she said she didn't think I was ready for such challenging work, my chest sunk; I was literally crushed.

"You know Sherry, these ideas are totally useless unless you work diligently with them."

Like a ripe juicy peach, her words hung in the air just out of reach. I had to try again; I was desperate to make something happen in my life. "Please," I begged.

Prema hesitated, tilting her head from side to side as if trying to see me more clearly. I don't know what she saw, but finally she said, "I still don't know that you're ready, but if you promise to make a real effort, I will tell you some of the arts of manifesting."

With an audible sigh of relief, I resumed my chest circles as she spoke to me.

"As I told you the day we met, intention is your most important attribute. If you want to accomplish anything you must first set your intention. The secret is to see the act as complete. See it finished. Visualize the end product." I waited eagerly for her to continue.

"Next, you say 'I will' and make a commitment to that end. Keep your intention and commitment before you at all times, like a mother bird tending her nest. Just as her eggs will eventually hatch, you will be drawn along to your visualized conclusion."

I was hanging on every word.

"As I've told you many times, *energy follows thought* is one of the principle laws of the Universe. The secret to manifesting is to work *from* completion…not *to* completion, but *from* completion," Prema repeated.

"Is this really possible?" It sounded like magic to me.

"You know, in the Bible Jesus says, 'All things are possible to those who believe.' This is not about believing in the Bible or even in Jesus, it's about miracles happening because you are open to possibility. If you don't put limits on what you or life can accomplish, anything can happen. Anything!"

"I can't tell you how much your view of life inspires me," I sighed. "But how come nobody lives this way? Even if it's true, it must be too hard to do."

"Your doubts are just what I'm talking about!" Prema snapped. "These limited thoughts, this devil that constantly whispers over your shoulder, 'you can't, you shouldn't, you've always failed before, be careful.' These doubts are negative forces inside of you that want you to stay the same. They control you by instilling fear. Whenever you begin to feel free, these negative entities are the ones who ask, 'who's minding the store?'

"You must be constantly vigilant. You must stand at the door of your mind and not let these thoughts in. Tell them to bug off. Refuse to entertain them. This will be the most difficult challenge of your life. You must fight for your freedom as if it's a life or death situation, because it is!"

I'd been shocked and chastened at Prema's intensity. If her intention was to wake me up and shake me out of my lethargy, it worked. And taking stock of my situation, though I felt a glimmer of hope, I was actually more fearful and overwhelmed then ever. As I promised her, I set her ideas in motion. And, as Prema promised me, it was the hardest work in the world.

I set intentions for everything, both the sacred and the mundane, and went about trying to change my limited thoughts of what was and wasn't possible. I certainly had nothing to lose.

I wanted my freedom. I wanted to save my own life. Now that I had the tools, I had no excuse for settling for the ordinary. I remembered her warning, "You must be constantly vigilant."

I felt like Sisyphus endlessly rolling that giant boulder up the mountain, only to have it fall back as soon as it reached the top. I felt despair, but surprisingly I also took inspiration from the myth. Sisyphus had been given this punishment by the gods who were jealous and upset with his extraordinary wisdom. I equated the difficulty of my struggles with the degree of wisdom I might obtain, and I redoubled my efforts.

When I told Prema about my struggles, she was very encouraging. Enthusiastically, I told her I felt a whole new world of possibilities and was truly committed to this work. She nodded as if she'd heard all of these promises before.

I tried to tell her how grateful I was to her for teaching me and wished everyone the good fortune of finding a teacher like her. But she deflected my praise. "A teacher can only teach as much as the student is willing to learn," she replied.

I was willing to learn anything and everything Prema had to teach. I'd never been a hero worshiper, but I realized then and there that I was seeing her as a model of who I could become. Lord knows I was desperately trying to find out what I was going to be when I grew up.

I knew it was presumptuous, but I felt pressed to ask, "Do you think," I began hesitantly, "that someday I might ever know enough to teach some of the things you are teaching me?"

The moment the words popped out of my mouth, I was embarrassed. But Prema just observed me for a few long moments. "It's very early to speak of such things," she said, narrowing her eyes.

I feared she'd feel offended by my arrogance and would ask me to leave. I knew at that moment how important these classes had become to me; they were literally a lifeline. Her silence was unbearable.

"There's someone I'd like you to meet," she finally said. "Go see my friend Narendra. He's a master of human nature. Whether or not you teach down the road, you must become familiar with the different types of people and how they learn. You have to begin to study human behavior so that you'll know how to help others.

"Yes," she nodded thoughtfully, "visit Narendra. Let's see if he sees teaching in your destiny. Most people think he's just a palm reader, a fortune teller, but don't get fooled by the appearance of things. He'll probably tell you he worked for the royal households in India, but he's actually descended from the great rajahs. He is a prince, a real prince, though you wouldn't know it by looking at his humble home."

CHAPTER 3:
AT THE CROSSROADS

T he next afternoon found me in my little yellow Volkswagen climbing steeply up Dennison Grade, a switchback road to the Upper Ojai. I reflected on the winding pavement, seeing it as a mirror of my life at this moment.

My clarity from yesterday was already dimming. My skeptical nature was clamoring at the gates. "You're going where?" it asked. "To see whom? To a palm reader? You must be kidding!"

As I rounded the last bend, the Upper Ojai took my breath away. Another long flat valley rolled out before me. Surrounded by mountains, the perfect patterns of the walnut orchards gave me a sense of order and security. Long narrow driveways branched off either side of the main road, disappearing under stands of tall eucalyptus trees.

Driving past the Sulphur Mountain turnoff, I continued on to Sisar Canyon Road, turning left into the narrow lane. Small houses lined the road, the only neighborhood tucked amongst the large ranches. At the end, up against the mountains, the pavement turned to dirt.

I stopped at a large metal barrier blocking the road. A sign read 'National Forest Land—No Trespassing.' As I got out to open the gate, the earthy pungent smell of sage bushes baking in the dry heat was like entering a sauna. I drove through, hopped out to close the gate, and then continued on.

I'd been down this road in the past when William, an ex boyfriend, had lived on the property. An old stone house deep in the canyon was originally the second home of a prominent Ojai family. Then in the late sixties a hippie commune built several small dwellings.

I searched for the cabin Narendra had described when I called on the phone. Each turn of the road revealed another small hideaway specifically created for privacy and retreat. I passed the stone pool carved into the mountainside. I remembered William and I skinny dipping on hot southern California nights when the Santa Ana winds blew torrid air through the canyon.

Passing the main house, built of large stones hauled down from higher up the mountain, I pulled up to a small cabin with a front made almost entirely of glass. Feeling like I was in hobbit land, I walked up the two short steps to the tiny porch. There was only room for a couple of rattan chairs with a small painted table wedged between them. The corners of the deck overflowed with red and pink geraniums in rough wooden planter boxes; the colors splashed brilliantly against their background of rustic wood and stone. Above the door hung a weatherworn plaque with an *Om* symbol carved in relief. I knocked lightly at the screen door.

A short man with round belly and equally round face opened the screen door and stepped out. His eyes, dark and deep, searched my face. He was dressed in traditional East Indian loose trousers and a long tunic shirt. In all white, he looked cool and collected as compared to how I felt in the searing summer heat.

He nodded to a chair and then sat down closest to the door. Narendra's presence was commanding. Without a word he took my hand and turned it over to look at my palm. He turned it this way and that then gently let go.

He started speaking in a polished, lilting Indian-accented English. Looking into my eyes, he proceeded to tell me things about my life, things I hadn't remembered for years. He also told me exactly what was happening right then. At first I was embarrassed that someone I didn't know could see right through me, but he recounted my experiences as if they were stories and I just a character in a book.

As he spoke, I heard my personal story unfolding like a coherent novel. Told in this way, I began to see connections.

Why I am the way I am. Why I do the things I do. And why I found myself standing at this crossroads.

"You know, this intense energy running through your body isn't understood here in this country," Narendra explained, shifting his weight in the chair. "Doctors here would say you are having panic attacks, or you are just high strung. They would probably give you some kind of tranquilizers that, by the way, wouldn't make you tranquil. They would make you catatonic as far as your will and intention are concerned.

"But in fact, this is a spiritual crisis. Hindu people are familiar with such conditions; it marks the opening of the *kundalini*. The kundalini is a vital energy that lies dormant at the base of the spine until it's called into action to be used in seeking enlightenment. Its opening or rising is a state to be sought after. In India we revere and take care of people who are in your position."

Having felt like I was going over the edge, I hung on every word. His information didn't change my condition, but I felt better just knowing what it was. It was the *unknowing* that had been the most difficult to deal with.

"We protect them," Narendra went on, "and give them the space to welcome this rare and unexpected visitor. They need time to go safely through the whole transformation process and let it unfold. We know the Spirit is moving through them and hope that whatever the outcome, it will be used for the greater good of all.

"You cannot predict how this force will be channeled by knowing the person before the process began. The kundalini rising is like filling the body with high-powered fuel. When released, it can cut through insurmountable difficulties and can also create unknown possibilities.

"Yogis do all kinds of practices to invoke this energy. They know that it brings them closer to the cosmic realm and higher ecstatic states. You seem to have come upon it by accident, an unwanted gift. But if you look back at your life, you may see that it is a natural outcome of who you were as a little girl."

I didn't know what to think; I could barely remember my childhood. It was very painful and, I felt, best forgotten.

"You used to have a dream?" Narendra questioned, but it was really a statement. I was startled. It was true that from the time I was about five, I would awaken in terror many nights with the same nightmare.

"You are walking down the stairs into a large pyramid…" I was shocked. How could he possibly know this? Was he reading my mind or what?

"Do you believe in reincarnation?" he asked.

I really didn't know. It would explain so many things and be an answer to the questions I'd always had about life's unfairness. Even as a small child I wondered why some people suffered and why some, who were clearly undeserving, seemed to have so many blessings.

"In India we believe that we have all lived many times before. Reincarnation is how the soul evolves. By going through a variety of experiences in different bodies, we come to understand that we are all one. And even when we become enlightened to that realization, the *bodhisattva* vow, which is the vow of the Buddha, makes us return again and again to help others until all are enlightened.

"You are at a crossroads now. You have the possibility of great wisdom and power, but you must decide if you will use it for the good of all or for your own benefit. It takes great sacrifice to be of service to others." He looked at me without judgment, but I felt he was wondering if I was up to the challenge.

He went inside, leaving me with this looming question. The stream from up the mountain burbled and the bees buzzed. The stillness and peace were a balm for my usually jagged nerves and racing mind. If this was the reward for traveling in the direction of service, I would gladly take it. But again, I saw how I was looking for something for myself, some personal benefit, and I wondered if I could ever be selfless enough to put aside my own desires.

Narendra came out with two steaming cups. *How,* I wondered silently, *am I supposed to drink that in this heat?*

"This is chai," he said, "black Indian tea mixed with spices that will cool you." I enjoyed the aroma and the taste.

As I set the mug down, he again took my hand and began to show me the different lines and mounds. He explained that the hand is a microcosm of the total person and a map of one's life. "Everything is to be taken under consideration—the shape of the whole hand, the texture of the skin, and the flexibility of the fingers."

He laughed as he bent my thumb back to almost touch the back of my arm. He told me this indicated I was very open to other people's energy and did not have a strong will of my own. "It would do you a great service to learn to set boundaries," he suggested.

Setting my hand down on the table, he explained further, "Palm reading is a good map to follow as you seriously begin to study human nature. But eventually, you will come to know people by merely observing their actions and checking your intuition. We are all very psychic, but with study and observation, you can open to anything you need to know about another person.

"But," he said emphatically, "you must have a practice that will still your own mind. Follow the message carved on the entrances of the great wisdom schools of ancient Egypt— 'Know Thyself.' Otherwise you will not know if what you perceive is your own projection or if it's really about the other person. Observe others carefully. To truly be of service takes a great understanding of human nature.

"Start reading people's hands," Narendra told me. "If nothing else you will make some friends. Everyone loves to hear about themselves, and holding hands is a good way to begin a relationship, no?"

He took my hand again and squeezed it. "Come visit me anytime."

Driving back down to the Lower Valley, I realized that Narendra hadn't mentioned anything specific about my future. But his perceptions and sincere offer to help me in my distress, and through my process of transformation, reassured me. With Prema and Narendra, I now had two springs of wisdom and knowledge to help me stay afloat.

CHAPTER 4:
PRIESTESS IN TRAINING

"I can see your meeting with Narendra did you a world of good," Prema said when I arrived the next afternoon. That was true. His explanations had taken the edge off some of my fears and helped me to see that I was going through a process that would eventually end. Now I was ready to get on with it.

"People throw the word love around very lightly these days," Prema remarked as we prepared to move. "Remember, love is one of the emotions awakened in the second chakra, but it is more of an earthly passion. The love that is awakened in the fourth chakra is different. This is the higher emotional center.

"Most people never go beyond the third chakra, if that. They may develop personal power, they may be able to use their will, and that is usually enough for the ego. We have too many examples of people who have developed their will but have no compassion."

Prema stopped to make sure she had my attention. "Going beyond that takes real sacrifice because then you are working for the world, not for personal gain. If anything, as you open this chakra you will seem to be losing some of the personal powers you've worked so hard to obtain. This is where we begin to develop real compassion. We begin to realize that we are all the same. We all say 'I'.

"Now place your awareness in the center of your chest. Gather your attention around your central axis. Begin to draw a tiny figure eight. As you draw the figure, breathe into it and let it grow larger and larger until you feel the eight you are making with the surface of your body. Now split your attention so you can feel the center, the tiny eight, and the large eight at the same time. Become very aware of your breath, let its rise and fall create the movement.

"Continue moving and imagine a small light in your heart chakra. Let it grow and radiate out in all directions. Use your inner vision and your breath to send it out."

Attempting to visualize these things was very difficult for me. I kept feeling a great resistance and I couldn't settle down. "Focus," Prema said, "and breathe deeply into that center point." I kept breathing forcefully, trying to ram my way through the barricaded inner doors that held my flickering light in check. Then suddenly...

I feel a push and seem to freefall from a great height. Plummeting into an even darker place, I'm completely disoriented and can't get my bearings. Gradually, I hear people crying and I feel their suffering, though mercifully I can't see them in the darkness.

I stumble to my feet and wander through a wasteland of despondent souls. As my eyes become accustomed to the lack of light, I come upon others who appear less needy, but still, I experience the poverty of their inner lives. I don't know if I've landed in purgatory or some alternate reality, but the amount of misery is devastating.

I'm overcome with hopelessness. I feel like the child I once was. That child wanted to save the world and feed all the starving children. She couldn't bear the unfairness and inherent sadness of human life. That child was still running, trying to protect herself from heartache.

I wander on. Overwhelmed by the atrocities I see, my heart literally shatters and falls to the ground. As I stop to gather the pieces together, the human race parades on past me. I see that most of the suffering is caused by humanity's ignorance; people fear and don't know of other possibilities. I'm ashamed that I've ever complained about my life. The phrase, 'There but for the grace of God, go I' echoes through my mind with each passing footstep.

Losing hope that I will ever find my way out of this living hell, I begin wondering what I can do to help. At that moment I hear a voice whispering, "The light, don't forget the light. Feel the light around your heart chakra and radiate it out in all directions." I see a dim light in the distance and follow it like a moth from this all-consuming darkness.

Opening my eyes, I found myself again standing next to Prema. A feeling of infinite gratitude overcame me.

Grateful to be alive after my frightening journey to what was surely the underworld, I worked a lot with the chest eights and other movements around the fourth chakra. The experience had been shocking, to say the least. Was it a vision? It felt so real. Prema told me that the practices we were doing had opened the doors to other worlds, and that I shouldn't lessen its impact by putting a familiar label on it.

Whatever it was, I hoped to learn to be useful if I ever encountered that kind of anguish again. Prema said that the only reason I got out of that place alive and emotionally intact, was my willingness to be of service. "You came back the moment you wondered what you could do to help."

The more I practiced, the more highly sensitized and vulnerable I became. Feeling other people's grief was unbearable to me. Once again I was overwhelmed. I stopped my movement practices, hoping this horror would disappear, but it only became worse.

The veil between my everyday world and that world I'd so narrowly escaped grew thinner and more transparent. I felt tormented souls grabbing at my psyche as if I could save them, but I didn't know how. I started to understand survivor's guilt.

One night I couldn't take it anymore. I called Prema to ask for her help, and she told me to meet her at Dennison Park. I drove slowly through the empty streets of downtown Ojai then floored it through the East End. The full moon played hide and seek with me as I wound my way up to the top of the grade, but I was in no mood for games. The people in my visions were haunting me.

As I came around the last bend, I found Prema waiting for me at the entrance to the campground. We never met away from her home, and I wondered at this unusual place for our meeting. We walked through the silent night, alone together, to a campsite with a view overlooking the Lower Valley. Prema directed me to collect some kindling and branches that she arranged in the fire pit then lit with a book of matches she took from her jacket pocket.

She looked at me over the flames. "You have to pull yourself together, Sherry, and learn the difference between compassion and sentimentality," she said sternly. "You can't be useful if you fall apart with every little whimper you hear."

I was shocked. I thought Prema was such a kind person, but now she sounded cold and uncaring.

"True compassion is not about being consoling and trying to make everything nice."

"But those poor people," I wept, describing what I'd seen.

"Pity does not help or change anything," she interrupted. "Think about what people really need. It's certainly not a lot of sweet sentiments about how it's all okay and how it will all work out in the end. Because it's not and it won't, at least not in any way that they will see. You need to help people be free, not comfortable."

I thought that she was harsh, and I argued that some people don't have the strength to change.

"Who are you to call others weak? How do you know? How will that image support them in any way? That's exactly the kind of thinking that takes the power of possibility away. Images kill! If you project your lack of faith on others, it robs them of their power."

"Well what can I do? I can't just stand by and watch."

"Everyone wants to *do* something," she sounded exasperated. "The road to hell is paved with so called good deeds."

"Well you're the one who keeps talking about being of service. I don't get you at all."

Breaking up more branches, Prema added them to the fire. The dry wood burned quickly. She didn't say anything for a long time. She seemed to be waiting for my agitation to calm down.

"You must remain detached and unemotional," she finally said.

"People will think I'm heartless," I cried. "And I don't know how to stay detached. People have been telling me their problems since I was a little girl, and it's almost killed me. What did they expect me to do? I was just a kid."

Prema let out a long breath. "Well, now we're getting somewhere. As a child you were vulnerable, but now as an adult you can learn to set boundaries so other people won't swallow you up. Just remember that being unselfish does not mean being self-sacrificing."

I started to cry again, this time with relief. Just the thought that I could get all these people off my back and out of my head lifted my spirits. There was a long string of them beginning with my family and right on through to these unfamiliar souls I was encountering in my visions.

Prema fished around in her enormous tote bag. "Here," she handed me a pad of paper and a pen, "write down the names of all the people you wish to divorce from your consciousness."

"That's such a cruel way to put it," I said. "That's really not very nice."

"You really have to get over this *nice* thing. You must become ruthless, merciless with your consciousness—it's your temple, your place of refuge and peace. You must keep it spotless and pure. Stand guard at your temple door. Don't open your door to unwanted guests. You are the keeper at the gate. Don't let in people who crush your spirit and stand in your light. This is your sanctuary, the holy of holies where you come face to face with the Spirit."

Put like that, I realized it was not selfish to want my own inner space. The flickering fire provided some light and luckily the moon was bright enough so I could see to write. I didn't even know where to begin. From the time I was very small, even grown adults had told me much more than I ever wanted to hear. They called me a wise little girl when I suggested different ways to look at their problems.

The paper was quickly filling; I turned it over and kept jotting down names from the past. I listed people who had hurt me, people I still worried about, and people who wanted something from me—all the people who still took up space in my over-crowded mind.

"There are many ways to release attachments and create boundaries," Prema said as she tended the fire. "Down through the ages, individuals and religions have used all kinds of elaborate rituals to accomplish these goals."

I started feeling hopeless again. "All that ritual rigmarole isn't my thing," I said. I really couldn't see myself doing the kind of rituals I was familiar with, and I had abandoned organized religion at an early age.

"Don't get stuck on the word," Prema warned. "A ritual is just a prayer that engages all your senses. Rituals from different traditions may not appear similar, but they do have the same components." She fanned the smoke away from her eyes. "Remember, the sequence of dance movements you and I do together can be called a ritual. And I, also, am not much into the rigmarole, as you call it. We can accomplish the same thing in simpler ways."

She had my full attention again.

"You are already familiar with the essential components of a ritual. First set an intention, then align yourself with a power larger than yourself and ask for help. Then do something symbolic to rally all your different selves together. Change can't happen if part of you is holding back."

I waited eagerly for the rest.

"Then repent…"

"Repent?" I interrupted. "That sounds religious to me."

"There you go again. You would throw out the possibility of help because you don't like a particular word?" She shook her head, "You don't even know what repent actually means."

To me it smacked of guilt-tripping, holier-than-thou cults.

"Repent merely means to change your mind, to think again."

"Oh," was all I could say. I was so embarrassed. Here I was asking for help, and all I did was put up one obstacle after another. I was surprised she would even continue talking to me. How could I be so ungrateful? I wondered if I really did want to change, or if perhaps I felt more comfortable holding onto the past.

"And the last and most important step in the ritual," Prema paused and looked at me meaningfully, "is to be grateful."

I hung my head.

"Are you ready to begin?"

I just nodded.

"First say 'May I be allowed to let go of my attachment to the people on this list, and may I have the strength and courage to guard my temple from unwanted intruders.'"

I recited her words out loud.

"Now drop the paper into the flames and watch it burn."

I did as she said. As the paper curled and turned to ash, I imagined the people leaving one by one from the crowded temple of my mind.

"And now say, 'thank you.'"

"Thank you," I said, then waited for further instructions.

When none came I looked up questioningly. Prema just passed her palms over each other in a wiping motion.

"That's it?" I asked incredulous.

"That's it," she answered.

She allowed a few moments to let it sink in then spoke again. "As I said, rituals can be elaborate, but all the outward embellishments are really just about focusing your mind and energy. If you know what you want and you can gather your attention, then your ritual can be very simple and quick."

I was amazed.

"Sweeping changes can often be accomplished in a very simple way. Bringing you out here tonight was actually unnecessary, but you were so agitated we had to do something pretty unusual to capture your attention.

"You don't have to seek out special places though. You can create rituals wherever you are. We used fire in this ritual, but you can choose other elements. For instance, you could bury your list in the Earth, or let it blow away on a strong wind. You could even just think of your intention and wash your hands. This is a very simple thing to do after a disturbing encounter. Just wash your hands and say, 'I release these negative feelings,' and watch them disappear down the drain.

"Another good way to sever attachments is to use a piece of string. Let it represent your connection with a person you don't want in your psychic space. Then cut it with a scissors."

"This all sounds like voodoo, does it really work?" I asked.

"Once again remember that the primary law of the Universe is that *energy follows thought.*"

We silently watched the embers die and then sat for hours as the moon floated above the valley and faded into the morning light.

Walking up the driveway the next afternoon, I heard chanting coming from the kitchen. Prema had mentioned that chanting while cooking was a great way to put love into food. I wondered how I would be able to focus with the mouth-watering aromas competing for my attention.

Meeting me at the door, Prema observed me closely. "Yes," she nodded, "you look much better. Last night you really let go of many useless ideas and emotions. Now that the excess baggage is gone we can proceed.

"Now that you're beginning to see the possibility of unselfish work, we can raise our attention to the fifth chakra. This is the center for self-expression, communication, and creativity. From here comes our ability to express ourselves in the world. From the throat chakra we can develop and store the energy and power to literally and figuratively sing our own song.

"You'll find this chakra behind your Adam's apple in the center of your neck. The circle we draw around the throat chakra originates in the muscles at the base of the neck. Circle in one direction and then the other. As before, concentrate on the center of the movement, then the tiny circle around the central axis, then the circle you are drawing in space."

I really had to pay attention to keep my nose facing forward and not turn or tilt my head. This was more difficult than I imagined. My lack of technique made me look like I was watching a tennis match.

"Now put your attention in the throat chakra and add breath to it. Inhale through the nose and exhale through your throat." The low whispering breath opened my air passages. It felt good to take a deep breath then fully exhale. I knew that I usually didn't breathe properly; I often found myself holding my breath or breathing very shallowly.

"Good," Prema said, "now add voice to the exhale with a low *sol* sound." I was self-conscious about singing out loud. I could barely carry a tune, but I did as she said.

"Do you feel the vibration in that area?" I nodded my head. "Excellent, continue," she encouraged. "Now increase the volume." I did. "More," she said. The vibration expanded to include my chest. "More!"

Singing *sol* over and over at the top of my lungs felt so good I didn't want to stop. I felt like an opera diva singing a dramatic aria, wringing out every last drop of emotion. I felt like a blues singer belting out a ballad. I felt like Janis Joplin wailing, "Take Another Little Piece of My Heart." I felt alive!

I don't know how Prema could stand it, but she stayed with me, prompting me to sing even louder. Finally I collapsed in an all out uncontrollable belly laugh with Prema laughing right along with me. When I recovered my breath, all I could say was, "That's amazing."

"Now as you practice, add sound as you do your movements around the chakras," Prema suggested.

"You mean just keep singing *sol* as I move?"

"No, no," she answered quickly, "certain sounds are associated with each chakra. *Sol* is the fifth note of the musical scale that we used with the fifth chakra. For now use *Do, Re, Mi, Fa, Sol, La, Ti* respectively from the first chakra on up. Later I will give you instruction on using vowel sounds. They were used in the Egyptian mystical traditions from ancient times to the present day. They're very powerful and best done with a guide to show you the proper way."

Of course I was intrigued and urged her to tell me more. "This is not the proper time, but I will show you something that's fun to do. Have you ever heard a *zaghareet*?" she asked.

I didn't know what she was talking about.

"A zaghareet is a sound that people, mostly women in the Middle East, make. It's a high-pitched ululation made with the tongue on the roof of the mouth." She showed me where to put my tongue and then instructed me to repeat *la la la la la la la* over and over until my tongue just started fluttering up and down on its own.

"Some people do it moving their tongue from side to side," she showed me, "but I prefer the other way."

I was following along with her. "Now you can change the pitch to higher or lower and also increase and decrease the volume." We sounded like a whole chorus tuning up.

"Why exactly are we doing this?" I finally asked.

"Oh," Prema laughed, "well, because it feels good."

"Is that why Middle Eastern women do it?"

"They do it for all kinds of reasons—to honor or welcome or greet someone, as a sound of approval, an exclamation of joy. You'll hear it used to encourage performers as they sing or dance. But people also wail and zaghareet in sorrow and mourning. It helps to move the energy when you're stuck in grief." I thought about how, in the West, we fight to hold back our tears and stifle our cries for fear of appearing weak and vulnerable.

"We've explored a whole variety of things today, but remember it was all around the fifth chakra which governs self-expression and communication. If your fifth chakra is closed down you will have a fear of speaking your truth, and perhaps you'll be overly shy. If it is too open, you'll speak excessively. You won't listen and no matter what you say, you won't really communicate with others.

"The idea is to create balance, and in this chakra that is done with sound." She then gave me some *mantras* and told me how to chant them. "They are ancient words of spiritual power, sacred sounds for the transformation of consciousness.

"Observe yourself in relationship with others. Make a study of how you interact. Do you really say what you want and get your point across in conversations? Try different ways of saying the same thing. It's how we say it rather than what we say that makes the connection."

I added the sounds to my daily practice. I also began hiking into nature by myself. I chanted the mantras as I walked the mountain paths surrounding the valley. I even went into town after months of avoiding it. I ventured out and looked around in stores and galleries and spoke to the shopkeepers.

I'd been living a very unsocial life since returning to Ojai. I was so concerned with myself and so involved in my own drama, that I wasn't interested in other people. It was a super effort for me to talk to strangers, but I walked into stores and struck up conversations so that I could observe myself as Prema had suggested. As I witnessed myself interacting, I thought, *this is me pretending to be normal.*

✳ ✳ ✳

We began as soon as I put my things down behind the fan chair. Our classes were not a social occasion. There was no small talk. I breathed deeply, settling myself.

"Place your attention in the center of your head behind your eyes." Prema's touch on my forehead was like an electrical shock. "This is the sixth chakra, sometimes called the third eye or the psychic center. Draw a tiny eight around this invisible point with your mind then make an eight with your eyes. Make it small or you'll strain the muscles.

"As you work with this center your psychic abilities will open and sharpen. You may know what others are thinking or what is about to happen. You will sense problems and often know intuitively what the solution is. These knowings will come in a flash. Whether you see or feel them, they have nothing to do with thought. They arise before you even begin to think.

"This ability is not to be taken lightly," she warned me. "If it is used for your own profit, you may get yourself into deep trouble. It's not a circus trick or a path to personal fortune. This is second sight, which allows you to know what is necessary in any given moment. It might be something simple like the plants needing water or a child needing a hug. Or it might be something much deeper, like what method of treatment would be best for a particular illness. Or it might show you what path to take to avoid an accident."

We spent the rest of our time together working with different methods of opening this chakra. Prema demanded complete attention. When we finished I was exhausted on one level, but my mind and awareness were crystal clear.

We went outside and walked around the property. Everything looked fresh and bright and super three-dimensional. My peripheral vision seemed so wide that I felt like I could see behind myself. We sat in the shade on the stone wall and listened to the silence. It was the moments like this, the ones you could almost miss in the clatter of daily life, that I was coming to cherish. I thought how much I had changed. The quiet spaces between the fireworks beckoned me.

Prema broke the silence, "You've seen that using these methods—movement, breath, sound, and visualization—can open and create energy in all the centers of the body. The intention of the priestess is to become an empty channel, a receptive conduit between Heaven and Earth. They come together within her and create what is truly necessary in the moment. Something real can be born. My teacher used to say, 'Become a son or daughter of the moment.' Allow the highest potential to manifest through you."

Gazing intently at me, Prema continued. "You have worked hard and made a good beginning, but this path gets more difficult as you go along. At this point you must decide if you truly want to continue. If you do, you must make a commitment and ask to be of service. Don't take this decision lightly. You will be asked to do things that go beyond what you think you are capable of."

Though she seemed to be discouraging me, her next words sounded like an invitation. "The Universe is waiting for the receptive."

She got up and left me to myself.

CHAPTER 5:
PATHWAY TO THE STARS

F ollowing the last class, I thought long and hard about my commitment to this path. It had already helped me and opened me to a much larger world. But I also thought about how strange and terrifying some of the experiences were. I wondered how much my commitment had to do with wanting healing for myself, or if I was really dedicated to helping others.

I arrived at class not sure of the answers to my questions. I still didn't have one clear and unwavering intention. All my little selves seemed to float around in my consciousness, each clamoring for attention. None of them wanted to sacrifice themselves for the good of all.

As always, Prema sensed my uncertainty. "Remember who you are in the dance," she reminded me. "You are the priestess standing between Heaven and Earth. You are equally receptive to the energies of both and are open as a line of clear communication and exchange between them."

Being reminded of this high vision of myself immediately dispelled my confusion. I did remember why I wanted to commit myself to this work. A feeling of solidity and purpose came to the front, and I was ready, aware, and able to be present.

"Now that we've worked with most of the chakras, and you are familiar with their functions and the energies they embrace, it's time to learn to move quickly and smoothly between them. You need to learn how to travel up and down your spine—it's the pathway to the stars."

Wondering what she meant, I felt like I was embarking on a journey deeper into the unknown. I had some trepidation but I was excited to begin.

"The undulations I am going to teach you are a very characteristic and integral part of Egyptian Temple Dance. They are the connecting link between the chakras. These movements allow you to pull the energy from the cosmos down through your body directly into the Earth and back up again. Think of the undulations as an elevator and the chakras as the different floors of a building. You are the passenger. You can stop at any floor and get off or continue riding up and down."

Being a very visual person, this image was an illuminating metaphor for me.

"Stand in correct posture with your eyes closed," Prema instructed, "and drop into your center." I immediately inhaled. I'd learned that the quickest way for me to get centered was to follow my breath into my lower belly. I pressed the air down through my lungs to my tummy then kept my attention there as the breath escaped upward. Repeating this action several times, I became very still. I could hear the water sprinkler outside and a little bird crunching around in the dry leaves.

"Become aware of the top of your head," Prema said when she saw I was ready to go on. "This is the crown chakra. A baby is born with this chakra open. The skull has not yet closed on top of the head. On a physical level, this allows for easier passage down the birth canal, and after that it gives the brain room to grow. In the first year and a half, the brain will double in size and then the bones will fuse closed."

Amazed at the wealth of knowledge Prema had at her fingertips, I wondered once again about her life and how and where she had learned the things she was teaching me.

"On a spiritual level the infant is still open to the unfiltered cosmic energy. When the skull finally fuses, the crown chakra usually stays closed throughout a person's whole life unless a conscious effort is made to reconnect to the higher self."

Placing her palm on top of my head, Prema said, "Now imagine an opening here. Feel the tingling and the warmth. Imagine light entering and filling your skull. Let it flood down through the throat chakra to your heart chakra. Usually this is as far as the cosmic energy will drop on its own."

Moving her hand down to my heart, she pressed gently. "There is a barrier here, like a circuit breaker, to protect the lower chakras from this massive energy. Unless the body has been prepared through meditation, movement, or prayer, this energy will blow the fuses of the lower or personal chakras. It would be like trying to put a thousand watts of energy into a lamp built for a hundred watt bulb."

"That's it!" I laughed out loud, "I blew a fuse!" She was perfectly describing the state that originally brought me to her and to this teaching.

"Exactly," Prema laughed with me, "this is exactly what happened to you. Because of a shock on an emotional level, the energy broke through into your lower centers, creating this uncontrollable feeling of too much to handle. This infusion of energy and light allows you to see your old fears and conditioning as they burn away. I know re-experiencing them is painful. I promise, though, that after the process of transformation is complete, the physical experience of the energy will become ecstatic and even orgasmic."

I couldn't actually believe that such a turn around was possible. Most of the time I was thinking that something was physically wrong with me and that mentally I was losing it. At times it was so frightening that I could barely breathe. Being here with Prema was the only thing that dispelled my fear.

"Now I want you to learn to move the energy around. Do you feel it vibrating in your heart region?" Prema asked.

I nodded.

"Use your ribs and imagine scooping this energy up and over your head. Then push it down past each vertebra, moving all the way down the spine to the coccyx. Now envision it flowing down your legs and pouring into the Earth through the Bubbling Spring, which is what the Chinese call the chakras in the soles of the feet. Keep repeating this movement until it becomes smooth, both physically and energetically."

At first my movements were jerky and awkward, but as I continued my muscles loosened up and my spine softened. In my mind's eye, I saw myself as one of those transparent fish that we had in our aquarium when I was a child. You could see right through them to their skeletons. I watched my spine ripple with the underwater currents.

Prema called me back from the watery depths. "Now open your eyes and let's continue the undulations as we travel around the room." Like two seahorses we drifted, our undulating spines propelling us through the space.

"These are beautiful movements with many variations. You can travel in any direction while undulating. Done in a circle, they create a spiral effect around the spine. On tiptoe they give you an ethereal look of floating above the Earth. And if you do an undulation and press down on your chest, not allowing it to move, you have a belly roll, which is an undulation of the lower chakras."

We moved around the room varying our undulations. Finally, it felt like real dancing. I watched our exotic-looking movements in the mirror. They had a dreamy, hypnotic quality to them. When Prema indicated that I should stop, I felt annoyed. I could have continued undulating right into eternity.

She ignored my displeasure. "The opposite movement is an *up* undulation, or what I call a body wave. It pulls the energy from the Earth, up through your body to be offered to the Sun. In the Temple Dance it is equally as important as the down undulation. Together these two movements gather, distribute, and circulate energy through the different chakras and then send it out again in a transformed state."

She showed me how to tilt my tailbone back and then push it forward to roll up the spine one vertebra at a time. The movements looked very erotic. "In the Temple Dance rituals we repeat these movements as many times as is necessary to pull the energy up. Of course for obvious reasons we don't do them over and over while dancing for an audience. Sometimes, though, we may do a single body wave to punctuate a series of movements, sort of like an exclamation mark."

Her movements were fluid as she illustrated. "Whether you're practicing the Temple Dance or performing bellydance, you use undulations to move the energy around in your body and connect the hip and chest isolations. You don't want a jarring, staccato movement; you want a nice smooth connection both energetically and physically. It should be seamless. This is what creates the mesmerizing snake-like quality of the dance."

We continued exploring a variety of undulations until my muscles ached and I couldn't take another step. I stumbled outside where we sat in my favorite spot under the oak tree. Prema tucked her feet up and continued our lesson.

"You've been learning to control the movement of energy throughout your body. Now let's talk about how you can use this knowledge for healing. Remember, the healing energy responds to attention, breath, and movement. And realize that by using these tools, you can actually access energy from anywhere in the Universe."

As I tried to take in this surprising information, Prema reached down to pet Krishna. When he arched his back and strutted away, she looked up at me. "If you can intuit what is necessary in the moment, you can focus on that particular quality or substance and draw it to you with your breath and movements. Think of yourself as the central receiving station for the healing pharmacy of the Universe. You can summon coolness from the Arctic Circle to relieve a fever. You can bring refreshing vitality from a jungle waterfall to revive a parched spirit. The peace and stillness of a mountaintop can come through you to quiet an agitated soul. Then you'll set your intention—and using your mind, breath, or touch—you'll project these qualities to wherever they are needed for healing."

I was inspired. Intrigued by the idea that distant energies and substances could be moved around like chess pieces, I asked, "Do most bellydancers know how to do this?"

Prema laughed. "Unfortunately, most bellydancers don't even know this is possible. Though Temple Dance and bellydance share the same origin and many similar movements, their intentions are not the same. One is focused inward for healing, the other outward for entertaining an audience.

"With practice, bellydancers can open the lower chakras and feel the release of old conditioning and the liberating flow of energy. That's why bellydancing is so addictive. But unless they study with someone who guides them through the process, the higher frequencies will not reach their lower chakras. They won't be able to bring a more inspired vision into the waiting world. This is the difference between the Temple Dance and the bellydance."

Usually a heavy sleeper, I was awakening in the middle of the night. Like an avalanche thundering down the mountainside, the energy in my chest roared. I was terrified I'd be buried alive before this transformation completed itself. My fear motivated me to practice the healing process Prema had given me.

One night I lay there in the dark trying to focus and steady my breath while searching for something in the Universe that could stop an avalanche. In my mind I scoured the planet to remember where in my travels I had felt most peaceful. Then I re-experienced a blissful day I'd spent in Death Valley…

I'm sitting on a large boulder in a canyon. Scanning the towering rock walls surrounding me, I suddenly feel an overpowering presence. When I realize I'm the only one around, my fear shocks me right out of my body. Looking down at myself, I'm reminded of old Chinese scroll paintings. In the bottom corner, the tiny person looking up at the vast landscape was meant to remind the viewer of our true place in the scheme of things.

It's so still, so quiet in the canyon, that as I turn my head I can hear the bones in my neck creak. The sound pulls me back into my body. Fascinated, I keep turning my head from side to side, listening. The movement soothes me like a lullaby. Feeling the presence again, I experience it as benevolent rather than as something to be feared. I soften. A sense of being protected envelops me, and I rest like a baby in her mother's arms.

Opening my eyes, I found myself lying in bed in my room. As my chest began to tighten, I closed my eyes again, trying to re-capture the vision. I couldn't see it, but I could sense it. I felt that I had found the doorway to ecstasy in that canyon. Reaching into the air above me, I gathered up that feeling and drew it down to me. I held it like a fragile ball over my pulsating chest, then with a quick short breath I inhaled it right through my ribs. The avalanche crumbled into powdery snowflakes floating lightly to Earth in the suddenly silent night.

I took the long way through the East End, so I'd have more time to pull myself together before class. The lack of sleep was exhausting me, but I was getting lots of practice with Prema's healing methods.

"You look like hell," Prema remarked as she held the screen door open for me. "And yet," she peered into my eyes, "I see a certain clarity that wasn't there before."

I told her about my middle of the night healing journeys.

"Yes," she nodded, "things often get worse just before they begin to turn around. Do you know that biblical verse? 'After the darkest night, joy cometh in the morning.'"

I loved it when Prema quoted wisdom teachings from various traditions. It helped me to realize that I wasn't alone in my difficulties.

Bringing us back to the moment, Prema said, "You began your studies by learning to find and open your chakras. Now with the undulations, you're beginning to travel from one chakra to another, balancing and creating resonance and harmony between the different centers.

"But to generate more energy is something else altogether. Think of it as going into higher gear or quickening the vibrations. If we did this work before balancing, we would just have more energy that we didn't know what to do with. Think of your own experience." She was absolutely right; I was living proof of her words.

"We also want to alter the *quality* of the energy. Think of it as changing the kind of fuel to fit the job. For instance, we need a subtler, more refined energy for healing than for getting the housework done. Think high octane as opposed to regular gasoline."

I wondered where Prema was going with this when she put her hands on her buttocks. "We use these muscles to create the movements. It may help to think in terms of a hydraulic process. We squeeze and release the tush muscles. This muscular energy converts to heat. Heat rises up the spine, turns to steam, and shoots up through the crown chakra."

She showed me how to contract and slowly release my gluteus muscles. "All your movements from the waist down will originate in these muscles. They're the largest muscles in the body, and we're asking them to do the most controlled and precise movements.

"In dance you want your body to be ready to receive, interpret, and respond to the music immediately. Remember, dance is a metaphor for life. We want to be prepared to respond to any stimuli in any moment."

We did hip downs, hip ups, hip forwards and back. "Remember," Prema said, "we're generating movements on a physical level, but the real action is on an energetic level. Work on this for a moment," she said as she disappeared behind me. I heard a rustling of things shifting around, then all of a sudden the sound of a drum filled the room.

"Don't turn around," Prema ordered. "Just respond to the drum."

After longing to dance to music, I was frozen. I couldn't remember a single step. What was I supposed to do?

"Listen to the drum. Listen with your spine, not with your ears. Your spine is the part of the body that develops first; it is the most primitive part of the body. Don't try to *do* anything, just let the vibration of the drum strike you in your back. You've learned to begin every movement from your back muscles, now instead of thinking about it, rely on the drum to initiate your movement."

I could feel the heavy *dum*, the deep vibrating sound of the drum when it's struck fully in the center. The sound hit my right buttock and pushed it up. The repeating pulse of the *dum* created a repetitive movement, first in my right cheek, then the left. They twitched right, left, right, left. I felt like a little wind up doll; my butt was taking off without me.

Prema slowly increased the speed and my hips responded in turn. "Don't get sloppy, keep moving from the muscles." The drumbeat finally got so fast I couldn't control the movement, so I just let go. My hips, rear, and belly vibrated to the drum roll. "Just let go and let your body shake. This is your shimmy. It's as *uncontrolled* as your isolation movements are controlled. That's how loose you want your shimmies to be."

Moving completely spontaneously, my lower body had a life of its own. The drum and my hips became one. I felt the sound was coming from within me.

"Relax into the movement. Keep your attention on the shaking of your hips and stay aware of your breath. Fill your abdomen with air, then your diaphragm, then your lungs. Now slowly exhale from your lungs…then your diaphragm…then your tummy."

My hips kept moving as if caught in a washing machine. Yet surprisingly, I was also able to control my breath—long, slow, even, and smooth, up and down my body. I felt like a volcano—churning underground, while the lava slowly and leisurely bubbled up to the surface.

Acutely aware of these two contrasting qualities of energy, I tried to keep my attention on both at the same time. Like two landmasses, they moved apart then butted up against each other, creating a building tension. Then something I can only describe as an earthquake occurred at the base of my spine. The room fell away, dropping me into a primal landscape…

Huge jungle plants cling to the slopes of the smoldering volcano, while a large serpent-like creature undulates toward me from beneath gargantuan leaves. I'm terrified.

"The kundalini is rising," I hear a voice echoing. "Don't be afraid, let her spiral around your spine...draw her up with your visualization and breath. See her dance like a snake to the sounds of the charmer...feel her climbing."

I experience a squeezing pressure, like a hug, as she winds her muscular way slowly up my spine.

"Only allow her to come as far as your heart chakra." I recognize Prema's voice but from very far away. "Now see her energy turn to light and radiate out in all directions."

My heart is bursting open. I feel joy, then ecstasy, then an overwhelming love and gratitude for being alive. It's so breathtaking that I could just die at this moment and be happy. But I hear Prema again, "Stay awake. Don't get lost in the sensation. Feel your feet on the Earth and draw your attention back down."

Slowly I became aware of the drumbeat calling me back into my body. And then I was very still, more still than I've ever been. Though the vibration in my chest resumed almost immediately, I didn't resist it. It had been a source of great fear, my reason for coming to Prema in the first place. But now I saw that the special energy running through my body held the key to this inexpressible joy and freedom. I was beginning to understand that I could be anchored in my body and also transcend it at the same time.

After giving me plenty of time to integrate my experience, Prema broke the silence. "Let the glow bathe your body. Become intimately aware of this feeling, knowing that it's always there for you to access. Remember, you have the keys now. In Arabic this feeling, this light, this blessing is called *baraka*. Turn to it again and again." Baraka, a blessing.

"Also in Arabic is the word *zikr*. The Sufis, the mystical sect of Islam, call their ritual practices zikr. It means to remember. I tell you these words because they can remind you in a simple and beautiful way of your experience today. If you remember the blessing and you turn to the light, you'll have the possibility of returning to this unfettered consciousness. Then you will be motivated to do your practices; they will be your path—your path is the way of dance. And if you are blessed, you will come this way again."

Zikr, baraka. Remember the blessing! How glorious! Crystal clear, I opened my eyes. "I couldn't possibly forget this magnificent feeling," I beamed.

"Don't get arrogant," Prema cautioned. "To remember and to have the will to turn away from what's familiar and comfortable is the most difficult challenge you'll ever encounter. This is not an ordinary experience. You won't get a lot of encouragement and support for going down this path. It can be very lonely."

Prema stood silently for several moments, letting me experience the magnitude of what she was telling me. I wondered if she felt lonely.

"When you first came to me, I told you that your most important attribute is the quality of your attention. I also told you that your intention would guide you. Practicing everyday, whether you want to or not, is the only thing that will develop your will to continue. No one else can do it for you. I can only point you in the right direction, guide you, and remind you if you begin to stray from your chosen path."

I was overwhelmed with emotion. I felt truly awake and alive. A door had opened, and I finally had a direction.

I found Prema waiting for me at the foot of the driveway. "We aren't going to dance today," she explained as I parked, "so let's walk as we talk." Turning up the lane away from the main road, we ambled along in the shade cast by the tightly spaced trees of the orange orchard. Bougainvillea vines crawled along the stone walls framing both sides of the unpaved road, their magenta flowers splashing vividly over the rough-hewn rock. Hummingbirds darted from flower to flower. Lizards kicked up dust as they scurried away from us. An army of large black ants marched single file over a downed branch. The scorching afternoon was ablaze with life.

I watched as Prema took in all the activity. Usually we met in her house and garden, and even there she appeared to be a very unusual character. Out here away from the environment she'd created, she seemed even more exotic.

"Have you always lived here?" I ventured, hoping that in this casual atmosphere she might reveal more about herself.

"Ojai is a very special place," Prema remarked, "I was led here several years ago and I love it." Just as I thought I was finally going to learn something personal about her, she laughed out loud with delight. We watched like voyeurs as two dragonflies zipped past us, mating in mid air. By the time they disappeared the moment for revelation had passed.

Prema turned her head toward me but continued walking. "We're coming to a crossroads in your studies with me. I've been introducing you to the beginning levels of the Temple Dance. Without this foundation you wouldn't have the possibility of learning anything useful. Let's take stock of what you're discovering.

"I think you're really understanding that you must literally put yourself in the proper position to learn. Mentally and physically, you must find and maintain a receptive mode in order to become a vessel for what needs to be born in this moment.

"You are beginning to realize that your body can create, receive, and transform energy from many places. Like a radio transmitter, it can send and receive across time and space, anything necessary in any given moment. You're learning to do this by setting an intention and using your attention, breath, movement, and visualization to transform energy.

"Getting down to the specifics of the dance, your mental attitude and your physical posture are where you must always begin. They mirror each other and reflect your intention to be present." Prema stopped walking and pulled herself up straighter. I immediately did the same.

"Once you are grounded, centered, and lifted, you have to align yourself around your vertical axis—it's a direct link between Heaven and Earth." Reaching up, she pulled her hand down the center of her body, tracing the line she described.

Taking a deep breath and exhaling with force, Prema continued. "We've worked on breathing consciously, freely, as everything in life comes in on the breath and leaves on the breath.

"With all of this preparation, we continued on to isolation movements for opening and unblocking your chakras. Then we added the undulations to move this free-flowing energy up and down. And finally, you've seen how the accents, snaps, and shimmies generate and increase the power."

Standing there in the middle of the deserted lane, with Prema demonstrating the movements, seemed both natural and otherworldly at the same time. I was thinking how rich and alive life is when everything suddenly stopped! Life just froze for a moment, shifting from a moving picture to a still photograph, capturing this special moment for eternity. Then suddenly, Prema started moving again, and it was hard to tell if that moment outside of time had actually happened. I was startled and a bit disoriented but even more alert.

"These are the basics, the building blocks," Prema went on as if nothing unusual had just happened. "The Temple Dance is a science of the body. After we're born our parents teach us things we need to know to survive in the physical world and in society, but it seems that we don't come with an instruction book for developing our full potential.

"You can go to college and get advanced degrees and never come into contact with this knowledge. People may only stumble across it when nothing else works in their lives, or when they are unable to reconcile some of the apparent injustices of life. They start to wonder *is there anything more? There must be another way.* Whether it's from becoming intimately aware of death or confronting heartache they can't bear, they become motivated. They ask questions. They seek. Otherwise they seem to be satisfied with the status quo."

Turning around, we started back down the road. Everything looked completely different heading in the opposite direction. I saw this as a visual metaphor for my experiences with Prema. I was still living the same life but nothing looked the same. Having Prema lay out our lessons in such an orderly manner and in an unfolding context, I could see her teaching as a systematic body of knowledge. I could see where I'd come from and catch glimpses of where I was going.

"Go home and consider what you've learned and how it has affected your life and understanding," Prema said as we neared her home. "Claim what you know as your own. Become responsible for what you have learned.

"You needed a map and someone who's been there before to help you navigate the inner terrain and point out the obstacles. You needed a guide to show you the way in. But I can't make the journey for you. Let your own wisdom make you stronger or it really isn't wisdom at all.

"As we go further into what you call *really dancing*, it gets more and more difficult to remember your intention and to be present. The music and movements are so sensual and seductive that we want to follow them anywhere, and we're impatient with the discipline of *remembrance*. We yearn to be taken away, to ride that magic carpet above the mundane life that surrounds us."

Prema's words painted a picture that closely resembled my original desire for learning to dance, but I'd followed her down an entirely different path.

"If that is what you're looking for, this is the time to find another teacher. On this path we dance to serve the moment. Be clear that this is your intention."

Krishna met us at the bottom of the drive. Prema reached down to pet him as I got into my car. "Don't come back until you're sure what you want," Prema called after me. I felt her eyes follow me out to the main road.

CHAPTER 6:
VISIONS AND VEILS

"Come on in and get ready," Prema called from the kitchen. Opening the studio door, I looked around for something unusual. When I'd called to say I was committed to continuing my journey with her, she sounded pleased and promised something special for our next class.

Entering, I held the door open for Krishna. Usually itching to leave when class began, today he jumped onto the high fan-backed rattan chair and curled up on the plush purple velvet cushion. "Oh, he loves veil dancing," Prema laughed, parting the beaded curtains.

I was thrilled. The veil dancing I'd seen in the park was the primary image I held of bellydance. When I imagined myself dancing, I was always swirling inside a transparent silk cocoon of a veil, my arms flung wide to the sky.

I could barely wait as Prema crossed the room. Opening a rosewood chest inlaid with intricate geometric mother-of-pearl patterns, she handed me a luscious turquoise silk veil. Placing a fire engine red length of fabric around her own neck, she showed me how to hold my veil—not too loose but not too tight either. A lyrical and haunting melody played on the stereo as Prema struck poses. I followed her as she moved her veil from one position to another around her body.

Prema draped the veil over her head then pulled the left side of it across her face leaving only her eyes exposed. "The veil epitomizes the mystery and allure of the Middle Eastern woman," she said. "It speaks to the power of beauty—a quality so strong that some feel it must be hidden or concealed.

"The veil can also symbolize other things, like wings or even the Spirit." Throwing her arms up, she did indeed look like she could take flight.

"It evokes the faraway untamed places of our imagination," she whispered. Stepping into a pose with her veil trailing behind her, she gazed off into the distance. I had the distinct impression that I'd heard her say those very words before while standing in that very same position, but this was my first longingly awaited veil lesson. Then I remembered the dream I'd had before my first meeting with Prema.

"Two of its main functions are to conceal and to reveal." Prema closed the veil then turned and opened one side, revealing a large hip circle that flowed into a figure eight. The effect of seeing only her hip move while the rest remained enshrouded, drew me deeper. I felt she was telling me a story though I didn't know the words. Then covering her hip while changing position under the veil, she paused and a most delicate shoulder roll emerged as she pulled the fabric aside. Continuing with her *now you see it, now you don't* technique, Prema revealed just how tantalizing it is to glimpse only the partial picture and imagine the rest.

Stopping for a moment, Prema glanced around the room as if gathering her thoughts. "Historically," she explained, "the veil is a symbol of the doorway to esoteric knowledge. Our veils must be lifted if we are to see Reality and become enlightened. There are many myths of the veil; the most famous is the tale of the Babylonian goddess Ishtar. Seeking to understand the meaning of suffering and death, Ishtar descends to the Underworld to confront Death himself. Guardians stand at each of the seven gates blocking her path. Ishtar is only allowed to pass through by relinquishing one of her seven veils. Each veil represents one of the illusions she must release if she is to understand the mystery of death and therefore of life itself. The tale of Salome and the seven veils evolved from this more ancient myth."

I was standing there spellbound by Prema's movements and by the tale she was weaving. "Begin moving," she urged me. "Use the veil to frame your isolations."

Draping the fabric in front of me below my hips, I watched in the mirror. Using it in this way exaggerated my movements, like a frame makes the painting inside seem more important.

"Now pull the veil up and frame your chest," Prema instructed. The silk concealed my lower body and complemented my subtle chest isolations.

"And now your head," Prema suggested.

With my hands holding the ends of the veil together above my head and the fabric draped under my chin, I could see how mysterious my head slides and circles became.

Prema pulled her veil up to the same position. "Don't forget your eyes," she admonished, sliding hers from side to side. Her already unusual eyes looked truly exotic framed in this way.

Trying to emulate her, I suddenly felt more relaxed than I had in ages. Noticing, like she always did, the change in my demeanor, Prema stopped our dancing. "You've just experienced why we do these eye movements. Originally they were part of the Temple Dance practices in which every movement had a specific spiritual and therapeutic healing function. Ancient Egyptian healers knew that moving the eyes in this way breaks up crystallized thought patterns.

"Most of the problems people have are a result of defective thinking. When we become stuck in thought patterns, we develop phobias or obsessions. Eye movement exercises were used to shatter these fixations. We in the West are just beginning to discover some of the practical wisdom that ancient cultures used as a matter of course."

Seeing my interest, Prema went on. "There's a relatively new therapy called Rapid Eye Movement Therapy. Patients are trained to follow the therapist's finger with their eyes while focusing on a particular thought that's detrimental in their life. Simulating the rapid eye movement state of sleep bypasses the defense mechanisms and releases the negative emotions. The uninitiated think of our eye movements as exotic dance detailing, but as you can see, the source is so much deeper."

As often happened when Prema saw that I understood from firsthand experience, she stopped further instruction so I could meditate on this new insight. Nudging Krishna over a bit, I sat down next to him and closed my eyes. I felt I had just learned something profoundly important.

Once again I found myself speeding out to the East End. Flooring the gas pedal, I soared out of the deep dip on Grand Avenue like a ski jumper. I was so excited to resume my veil training that in my mad rush to get there, I almost hit a quail family racing across the road. Once again I was completely overlooking the moment. I laughed at how the Universe had sent me a frantic little quail family to mirror my frenetic behavior.

When I arrived I told Prema about the quail. "Ah yes," she said with a knowing smile, 'it's *all* done with mirrors." She wouldn't elaborate, and I was to contemplate her words for years.

This time Prema held out a basket overflowing with veils of myriad colors and patterns, allowing me to choose the one I wanted. I pulled out a fuchsia silk with gold embroidered borders cut from an old Indian sari. Placing it around me, I savored the feeling as I drew the smooth fabric across the back of my neck.

"Today," she said as she lifted a sequin-trimmed white chiffon from the basket, "imagine the veil is a diaphanous extension of yourself. Think of it as your spirit or wings that help you fly. Use your wrists to capture the air underneath it," she showed me. "Let it billow like a sail; the loft will keep the material from wrapping limply around your body."

Prema made it look so easy that I thought mastering my veil would be a snap. But each time I tried, it kept getting caught around my head. I couldn't find the edges and the more I pulled at it the bigger the veil seemed to grow. I felt like I was trying to punch my way out of a paper bag. It seemed to expand even more until I was positive a tent had collapsed on top of me. Though I may have been bigger and stronger, my veil proved a worthy opponent. The harder I tried the more uncontrollable it became.

When I finally got the damn thing off my head and saw Prema barely stifling a laugh, I was about to explode. "It must be the *djinn*," she remarked, trying to diffuse the situation.

"What's the djinn?" I asked, still flustered.

"You mean *who* are the djinn," she answered.

Seeing that I was about to lose it, Prema explained, "Bedouins, the desert dwellers of the Sahara, believe that djinn are shape-shifter spirits who like to make mischief. They attribute all kinds of mishaps and mysterious happenings to the djinn. But the djinn can also help you.

"This is where the word genie comes from. Those genies are always quite annoyed at being cooped up for centuries in those cramped magic lanterns," Prema teased. "But they do end up granting three wishes!"

She urged me to imagine wings and give the veil work another chance. Relieved that I had an excuse for being so clumsy, I was willing to try again. I spoke to the djinn in a soothing voice, sympathizing with them for their unfortunate and crowded living situation and asking for their help with my veil.

It seemed to work; I finally felt the air under my wings. Soon I was twirling the veil around my body and gliding around the small studio. Feeling confined, I was afraid I would knock the treasures off the walls. Prema opened the screen door and out I flew like a trapped butterfly. I ran around the garden, my veil wafting lightly behind me.

I sprinted down the driveway past my parked car and out onto Thatcher Road. I came up short as a red sports car shot past me. Sure that I could take him on, I raced down the road yelling for my djinn to help me. Feeling a push on my back, my feet left the ground…

*I'm flying, free, wild, and gaining on the car in front of me.
I catch the driver's look of shock in his rear view mirror. Seeing
myself through his eyes, I immediately fall to Earth.*

And then I was running again, so fast I stumbled. Slowing
to a walk, I found myself almost to McAndrew Road but not a
bit out of breath. Making my way back, I contemplated the
power of thought. Prema continuously reminded me that one of
the primary laws of the Universe is that *energy follows thought.*
Now, even though I kept having experiences that proved her
right, my so-called rational mind scoffed at believing I had
actually flown. My experiences of late were definitely out of the
ordinary, but did this mean they weren't real? Why, I wondered,
would I hold so tightly to a view of life that made me unhappy
and didn't acknowledge the miraculous?

I could barely wait for the next class. I spent hours whirling
around my living room with the royal blue veil Prema lent me. I
became entranced with concealing and revealing every square
inch of my body. I was practically drunk with the knowledge
that I could create such beauty. I could almost have left my car
at home and flown out to the East End with my veil soaring
behind me. I must have looked like a mad woman when Prema
answered her door. Mercifully, we got right into it.

"Think of the veil as clothing," Prema said, showing me
how to make a skirt by tucking and draping it as I spun. Then I
copied her as she folded and pleated the silk, sari style. We
assembled several different looks while continuing with our
dance movements.

The most difficult and impressive creation had to be the
turban headdress that we wrapped around our heads and under
our eyes. "Continue spinning," Prema instructed as she told me
where to place my hands and how to anchor the fabric. When I
finally stopped turning and let go, I was utterly dizzy but the
headdress was completely secure.

"Magic!" I exclaimed, giddy with excitement. "I'm really
making magic." Prema smiled at my enthusiasm.

She showed me how to flip the veil over and under my extended arms to simulate different sleeves, accentuating my arm and hand movements. "Many of the dance gestures of different cultures were created in the royal courts to show off new and elaborate clothing styles. For example, classical Persian dance is all about posing and modeling the long silk embroidered sleeves that hung to the floor."

Prema showed me many ways to wrap the veil on my body. She said I should be mostly concealed at the beginning of a dance and then slowly emerge as a butterfly from a cocoon. Each unwrapping of my veil revealed a new movement and evoked different emotions. Then she taught me to make tents and cones and various other frames to accentuate my torso movements. The sculptress in me was thrilled to create these structures I could dance inside of. Of course the djinn made a hasty return to toy with me, and I knew it would take much practice to learn to do these movements smoothly.

My arms were getting tired, so Prema let me sit while she continued dancing with her gold striped veil. Watching the master at work, I became hypnotized by the metamorphosis from one visual image to another. Seeing how fascinated I was, Prema said, "These are all very interesting tricks but you see them done all the time. They've become a cliché. Veil dancing can be the most personal part of a dancer's performance, revealing her essence. Improvising with your veil will allow us to watch you create a variety of pictures as you explore. Then the quality of your dance will be completely different from just running through a choreographed set of veil tricks."

"It'll be years before I'm able to do that," I moped, "I wouldn't know where to begin."

"Nonsense," she chided, "you were doing fine before. You just need to cultivate a relationship with your veil. Don't think of it simply as a piece of fabric that you toss around like you're folding laundry. It's a living being. Use your imagination, and the veil will come alive and become whatever you wish it to be."

"Like what?" I wondered aloud.

"Are you willing to explore?" she asked.

"Why not." I rose from my chair. I was getting used to being a fool in Prema's wild world. I knew by now that when she critiqued me or laughed, she was laughing with, not at me. Often when I was embarrassed by my awkwardness she reminded me, "To put yourself in the position of a beginner, for the opportunity to bring beauty into the world, speaks of the quality of your Being."

Prema put on a haunting piece of music; the flute and the violin wove a spell around each other. "We've already talked about the veil as wings or as spirit. What about our nature friends? Can the veil make waves?" Showing me how to follow through with a flick of her wrist, she created the crest of a wave.

Once again the all-pervading feeling of déjà vu overcame me—I felt I had experienced this moment before. Then the dream I'd had the morning of my first lesson with Prema rushed back clearly. I wanted to ask her for an explanation, but she was urging me to follow along with her.

"How about a rainbow?" She was wafting the veil from side to side over her head.

"Can you whip up energy like the wind? Like a gentle breeze…an erratic gust…or a tornado?" Prema progressed from lifting the veil lightly, to flicking it sporadically, to thrashing it furiously around her body. I could hear the fierce wind howling through her veil.

"Now can you evoke the look and feeling of a waterfall…or a fire?" All the while she exaggerated her movements so I could see what she was doing. Her veil conjured up living entities. They morphed from one into the other leaving me spellbound.

Enthralled, I copied Prema's every move. When I captured them correctly, I felt I was communing directly with nature. I could feel the shift in the atmosphere as the different elements were called into manifestation. Merging with my veil, I was whirling the Universe into being.

Each time I was sure I had exhausted all possibilities, a new movement would emerge. Prema laughed, "I'm still discovering new moves after forty years of veil dancing. Creativity is unlimited, infinite. We could tell the whole story of creation with our veils."

Our afternoon of visions and veils slipped away. My arms were limp, and I was humbled by Prema's generosity in spending so much time with me. Surprisingly, when I thanked her she said almost shyly, "A teacher is always grateful for a receptive student. I'm filled to the brim with knowledge to pass on. I need to make space to learn more. It's a continuous process of learning, teaching, then learning some more."

She'd shown me a world of such beauty, I wanted to assure her that I didn't take it for granted. I tried again to thank her, but she said it was the quality of my attention that allowed her to impart certain things. She said that I should be grateful—not to her, but to the Spirit that had allowed me to come into contact with such a beautiful practice.

Half an hour early, I parked at the bottom of Prema's driveway. I found myself arriving for class earlier and earlier. Driving from home felt like a pilgrimage; I couldn't wait to get to the holy temple. Just being in the proximity of the studio made me happy.

I strolled up and down the lane through the orchard waiting for my shrine to open. I'd never been one for hero worship, but in my mind Prema was becoming a mythical figure in possession of mystical secrets. I couldn't get enough.

"Have you been working on your paddle turns?" Prema asked as I put the veil around my neck. Last time she'd promised me that if I could spin easily in both directions without getting dizzy, she could show me dozens of veil movements done simply by changing arm positions.

All week I was a spinning fool. Working up from four count spins to eight, then finally sixteen, I gave the whirling dervishes a run for their money. This was no easy feat as I was prone to dizziness after just a couple of turns. A few nauseous moments had sent me running to the bathroom, but the sensation passed by the time I got there.

Now I was spinning pretty confidently and proudly showed Prema. She looked surprised and pleased. She reminded me to keep my knees unlocked so I wouldn't bounce up and down, but would remain level. "Well then," she nodded, "we're ready to go on." Changing to a sheer, green, iridescent beauty from the basket of veils she offered, I flung it over my shoulders with satisfaction.

"Let's review and then add on," Prema said, unfolding yet another vividly colored veil, the rich purple fading into lighter shades of lavender. I followed her as she spun around. She held the veil behind her in different positions—both arms up in a high vee, then out to the sides, then into diagonal lines right and left. With the veil swirling around her, each change of arm position made a completely different picture. Each transformation was captivating. I stopped to watch because she was just so breathtaking.

"You haven't seen anything yet," she winked as she *toreadored*. Like a bullfighter, she whipped the veil over her shoulder. Repeating the same arm positions with the veil in front this time made the movements look completely different. Next she held one hand behind her back creating the look of a one-shouldered dress with a single long fluttery sleeve.

Prema scooped one arm under the right side of the veil and spun several counts to the left. In an instant she reversed the scoop to bring her left arm under as she changed directions.

The effect was mystifying, and I had to watch very carefully to see how she did it. It really seemed like magic. Just when I thought I was getting it, she quickly moved her arms up and down on the diagonals. She looked like she was framed in a giant rose.

Spinning seamlessly through an evolving series of arm positions, Prema was mesmerizing. One picture flowed into the next. Time slowed down and I understood how the dance itself is a gift. Watching her lifted me out of ordinary time and space. I could relax, take a breath, and feel my own life in Beauty.

Prema came to an elegant pause with the veil wrapped around her and her head dropped back. She looked so peaceful and vulnerable. "Life just moves too fast," she said, stepping out of her pose. "We're overwhelmed with busyness. Whatever can help slow us down enough to feel our own life is a blessing.

"Creating an unfolding picture captures the audience's attention, and as we know, attention is the doorway to the present moment. Beauty is also one of the pathways to the here and now. If you can bring someone to the doorway and they are willing to just take a single step, they can enter a whole new world. Rumi, the great mystical poet said, 'The sole purpose of Love is Beauty.'"

"You might contemplate that," she added as she folded her veil and left the room.

At home I practiced my veil dancing, but my mind was busy with Rumi's words: "The sole purpose of Love is Beauty." At the moment Prema said it, and filled with the experience of true Beauty, I understood what the phrase meant. Yet later when I tried to think about it, I just didn't get it. What kind of love? What kind of beauty? How were love and beauty related? Did Rumi mean sole or soul? The words held a great promise that I was obsessed with finding again.

Believing somehow that these words were the key that could pry me open and release *my* soul, I wandered Ojai's mountain paths searching for understanding. Mostly my mind just ran amuck, but sometimes repeating the line over and over worked like a Middle Eastern version of a Zen koan. Periodically my mind would stop, I'd awaken to the great beauty surrounding me, and I'd stumble on the meaning once again. The world opened and I could feel the benevolence of the Universe. But it was an elusive state.

I came to believe that Love and Beauty are each a Presence—entities or qualities that live in and pervade the very air that we breathe. At times of grace they come together like twins or lovers. We are always in their presence but we are truly blessed when we recognize them.

To feel that my dancing could evoke such a state gave me the determination to commit myself more fully. I decided to call my dance practice the Way of Beauty. In my dreams and visions I saw myself as a messenger of Beauty, dancing for a waiting world.

It was one of those sparkling clear days when everything looked brand new. Pulling into the driveway, I saw Prema sitting under the oak tree with her beading tray in her lap. She rose to go into the studio for our lesson, but I asked if we could stay outside for awhile. I wanted to tell her what a gift she'd given by quoting Rumi's words to me. I told her about my insights and my vision of myself as a messenger of Beauty. I was moved to see Prema's eyes glisten as she said softly, "Now you've given the gift back to the giver."

I tried again to express my gratitude, but Prema cut me off. "Now you're ready to begin the small class that I teach here on Wednesday nights for my other serious students. Besides learning deeper levels of the Temple Dance, you'll learn more advanced bellydance technique. We'll also work on choreographed dances and performance skills."

Seeing my excitement, Prema warned me that these subjects that intrigued me so much would also make it even more challenging to stay in the moment. "There is a blessing and a curse in having a practice that feels so good. It simultaneously makes you want to practice, *and* it's easy to get lost in the sensation. Remember, our intention is to stay aware."

In my desire and yearning to dance, I was more than willing to take on that challenge. Prema set one more intention for me to follow. "Your most important job will be to observe how the other students approach learning. We think we know other people, but it's usually just an image based on very limited information. We fill in with our own projections of how we would act in similar situations; and we don't really observe who is in front of us. How can we hope to be of service if we can't see clearly?"

I saw there would be no rest on my journey. I wouldn't be allowed to bask in my personal pleasure. Prema was already setting my next task before me.

INITIATION II:

THE WAY OF BELLYDANCE

CHAPTER 7:
TEKKA DUM, TEKKA DUM

Wednesday evening I impatiently sped down the road to the East End. In my haste I barely saw the captivating landscape right in front of me. Turning wide into Prema's driveway, I once again narrowly missed the century plant. Congratulating myself on learning enough to be invited to the group class, I forgot her warning to drive slowly. Prema was afraid Krishna wouldn't get out of the way of cars coming and going. I felt ashamed, and lucky that he was nowhere to be seen.

As Prema requested, I came early so she could give me individual instruction before the other students arrived. Walking quietly up the driveway, I heard the metallic ringing of finger cymbals. As I opened the door Prema handed me four cymbals, two for each hand. "These are called *zils* in Turkish and *zagat* in Arabic," she said as she showed me how to place them on my fingers. "You'll not only become a dancer, you will be a musician as well and learn to accompany yourself as you dance."

Krishna was meowing to be let out. Opening the screen door, Prema explained, "Since he's blind he's super sensitive to the sound." Krishna bolted to freedom.

"Originally, temple dancers played finger cymbals to chase bad spirits out of the temple," she told me as I stretched the elastic finger loops onto my thumbs and middle fingers. "Cats were kept for the same reason. They're highly sensitive to things we can't see or hear."

I turned toward the sleek black feline sculpture holding a prominent place next to the fountain. Seeing my curiosity, Prema introduced me to Bastet, the cat goddess. "She holds a very high place in the pantheon of Egyptian gods and goddesses. She was responsible for joy, music, dancing, and healing. She also protected Ra, the Sun god, by battling serpents that threatened him. Cats were sacred; killing one was punishable by death." I thought of Lily, my little prima donna cat. I was sure she was aware of her royal heritage.

Turning to face me again, Prema demonstrated the correct position for my hands and how to strike the cymbals. "Keep them close together and use a light touch so you can increase the speed. Hold them so they can speak to each other, and allow the pair on each hand to caress one another. Simply play *right left right, right left right.* The zils say *tekka dum, tekka dum.* This basic rhythm is often called *longa.* Begin moving with this simple pattern and then you'll be able to go on to more complex rhythms.

"You can also use the same pattern on the *dumbec*, the Middle Eastern drum. I'm teaching you to play the rhythms the same way the drummer does." Tapping out the rhythm on her tummy, she showed me how it would be played on the head of the drum.

"You have to learn the rhythms if you're going to dance to them. Each rhythm is from a different country, region, or tribe and calls down the specific spirit that protects that group. Each spirit has definite and particular habits, likes, dislikes, colors, clothes, and even food and drink that it favors. Rituals to invoke, placate, and honor these spirits include offering them their favorite pleasures. The dance movements mirror the way the spirit itself moves when taking physical form. Most dancers think that this is only true of African dance, but bellydance is greatly influenced by the dances of other cultures." Hearing the sound of cars pulling into the driveway, Prema said, "We'll speak more about this another time."

Prema introduced me to Felicia, Rachel, and Emily as they each came in. They quietly got ready then began playing their cymbals. I took my place in the small circle with Prema and the three women. I recognized two of them, Felicia and Rachel, from the day at Matilija Canyon. I began playing tentitively and though I tried to keep my mind on the cymbals, I was fascinated with the jingling coin scarves and glittery clothes they were wearing. My fingers stumbled.

As we played we began moving our arms. I stopped and cursed myself with every mistake. "Just keep playing," Felicia commanded. "It's just wasted energy to judge yourself, begin anew each time. It's like learning to rub your tummy and pat your head at the same time. You can do it if you pay attention." I felt myself bristle. I didn't like being told what to do by a stranger, and I felt dismissed like a naughty child.

After moving through more intricate rhythms, which I totally butchered, we began doing the basic movements I'd learned. I couldn't move and play cymbals at the same time, but I was loving it anyway. Prema switched to more upbeat music, adding steps and spins. Finally, I was fulfilling my dream of dancing like the bellydancers I'd seen in the park. They had been my original inspiration.

To learn the Temple Dance, I'd had to put aside my vision of dancing with wild abandon. The strict discipline had shown me worlds I hadn't even imagined, but I still longed to let go and just dance joyously. It had taken so long for me to get to this point where my experience began to meet my expectations. I wanted to savor every moment.

In the evening light the exotic treasures in the studio conjured images of a nomad's tent on the edge of the desert. Sequins twinkled like stars, and swaying crystal beads shot flashes of aurora borealis lights across the room. The sculptures of the gods and goddesses came alive, their heads turned in unison as we entertained them. The other dancers in their costumes and the lingering scent of incense fueled my imagination. Music from the stereo and the hypnotic sound of the finger cymbals transported me…

Looking beautiful in my costume of silks and coins, I dance before an adoring audience. I love being the center of attention.

"Circle to the left," a voice brought me abruptly back to the room. Felicia was looking at my hips and indicating that I was going in the wrong direction. I looked helplessly at Prema.

"Felicia, there's only one teacher in the room. If there's correcting to be done, I will do it," she said pointedly.

"But she was falling asleep, I only..." Felicia began to make excuses.

"No!" Prema repeated quite sternly. "Try and learn something here. It's not all about technique. I could have helped Sherry more by waiting for her attention to stray even further away. Then when I called her back, she'd be clearly aware that she was absolutely not present."

I felt vindicated that Felicia was the one put in her place, but that only lasted for a moment. "You completely forgot yourself," Prema admonished me. "You were off somewhere in a fantasy world. Remember, this is training for life. How could you be of use if something happened? Even now you're having trouble getting grounded."

This was true. I was having trouble letting go of my desert vision. My mind cleared for a moment, but then I began sorting through a mix of thoughts and feelings—calling myself stupid, happy that Felicia had been reprimanded, thinking about what clever thing I should have said to defend myself. Would I ever learn to stay aware?

"Those thoughts are all useless," Prema said as if she knew what I was thinking. "We've already moved on." And indeed we had. They were working on their hip articulations and though my hips were following along, I was still deep in the previous moments.

The class that I had so looked forward to continued, but I was stuck in the past. I realized how much of my time was spent in the land of *what I should have done or said, what I wanted to do, or where I wanted to be.* The past and the future were both well known to me, whereas *now* was a novel concept.

If I hadn't studied privately with Prema, I wouldn't have had this profound insight into myself. I would be hopelessly lost in the fantasy of the situation with no hope of learning anything beyond the physical technique of the dance.

The class went on. We shimmied. We danced a small sequence. In another frame of mind I would have been thrilled, but I was still struggling with this inner lesson. The class finished in a circle. We ended as we began, arms circling overhead then coming to rest with hands in prayer position or *namaste*.

I went up to Prema, wanting to ask some questions about movements I'd found difficult. "You got the real lesson for tonight," she broke in, "sometimes what we think is the point of the class is very far from it. Contemplate the movements of your mind rather than the steps we worked on. Go over them like a map and see where you took the wrong turn. Find out how to get back on course when this happens again. Because it will."

As I left the house, Rachel caught up to me in the driveway. "She's always like this," she said looking back over her shoulder at Felicia. "She thinks she knows everything. And especially since she came back from studying in New York. She corrects us all the time, like she got the truth directly from Isis herself."

"Thanks," I said turning toward my car.

I opened then closed the door without getting in, not yet ready to concentrate on driving. Walking down the driveway then on down the road, I searched the pitch black, star-studded sky. With no streetlights in the East End, I could see every last one. Since returning to Ojai I hadn't even noticed them. What a metaphor for my life. I was so distracted with the bright lights of life—the glitter, glamour, and drama on the surface—that it blinded me to the amazing reality right behind it.

A shooting star raced across the sky and dropped almost at my feet. The intoxicating fragrance of the orange blossoms and the warm Santa Ana breeze from the south brought me right back into the present, and I basked in the richness of it. Reality exceeded my fantasies of what I thought life could and should be. Each moment was new and held the promise of endless possibility. With Prema's classes bringing me to these realizations, I was on the right track at last. I felt like I had come home.

When I arrived at Prema's house, the pungent aroma of fruit and sweet spices—cinnamon and nutmeg—greeted me at the door. "Chutney," she said in answer to my sniffing. "It's an East Indian condiment made with fruits or vegetables. I bottle my own and age it for a year.

"Let's sit outside." She led me to the shade under a huge California oak. We sat, me on an old wooden chair, Prema on a broken limb. With her legs tucked up under her and her hair shining like copper from the sunlight filtering through the branches, she looked like a leprechaun.

I was filled with questions and wanted to blurt out all that I'd discovered since Wednesday night, but Prema put her finger to her lips. We sat quietly and I became aware of a crackling sound behind me. I turned to see a most majestic peacock, brilliant blue and green tail feathers spread in full array. He was less than ten feet behind me. How could I have missed him? We'd walked right toward him. I'd been so full of myself that I once again missed the amazing spectacle right before my eyes.

I realized now that I spent most of my life asleep. I was always thinking of somewhere else or waiting for my life to happen. How much had I missed that was right in front of my eyes? It was devastating to think that I had blindly overlooked most of my life.

When I told Prema my thoughts, she smiled with a hint of sadness as if she, too, mourned all the lost moments and un-manifested potential. "Most people never wake up. But that's not really any consolation, is it?"

I silently vowed to work diligently to stay awake and not lose any more of my moments. With a loud cry, as if affirming my decision, the peacock closed his tail and exited stage left. I chuckled to myself imagining he was very proud of his part in my drama.

I began describing my experience after Wednesday night's class. Prema particularly noted the timing of the shooting star. "You're becoming attuned to the natural world," she said pensively. "Your encounter with the star, and then again today with the peacock, is important. You're beginning to see that the Universe is responsive." She paused, then said with emphasis, "That's why you must always have a question."

"A question?" I echoed.

"If you keep your question in front of you, you'll be aware of life responding. This will help you see that the Universe isn't a cold and impersonal place, but a friend that you're in dialogue with."

"What kind of question?" I asked. "It would have to be something pretty profound for the Universe to bother answering me."

"No, no, no…" she laughed. "You can ask anything, but it must be a sincere question pertaining to the moment. It's not for fortune telling. Pose it as a yes or no question. And remember, *yes is yes, no is no*, and *maybe is no*. Trust in the answer, then heed the advice."

"How will I know or be told?"

"It can be in many ways," Prema answered. "A feeling inside of release or freedom, a physical reaction—maybe a slight shiver of fear. Or as you've just been experiencing, the answer comes as a shooting star or a peacock folding its tail. Learn to trust your feelings, your intuition is your inner compass, your natural guide. As the mythologist, Joseph Campbell says, 'Follow your bliss.'"

I thought about the countless times I'd second-guessed myself. I didn't do what I felt like doing but did what I thought I *should* do. Those decisions always turned out badly because I didn't have any energy behind them. I procrastinated and couldn't find my way, or found many things blocking my progress. Later I would see someone else doing what I'd really wanted to do, and I'd feel once again like I had failed myself.

I'd denied my intuition so many times, and it was buried so deep that I could barely hear it.

I made another vow to myself. I promised to remember to always have a question. I'd listen to that still small voice and follow it. I'd take the risk, accept the consequences, and see how things worked out.

I asked about Felicia.

Prema seemed to be considering whether to discuss her. Finally she said, "Everyone in the class wants to teach the dance at some point. Each has her strong points but also her shortcomings.

"Some students come with cups so full that there's very little space to add anything new. Others have cups that are very empty, but that's also not the best position for learning. If you have very little in your cup and you don't have enough self-esteem to claim what you already know, then any new perceptions have nothing to stick to," she explained. "They just keep dripping through the holes, and you're always dependent on the teacher or the outside world."

Shifting her position on the limb, Prema said, "There are so many obstacles to learning. Some students have too many set ideas. Others are attracted to glamour, they always want bigger, better...anything but what is. Sound familiar?" She raised her eyebrow, and I responded with an embarrassed laugh. "And then some people have too much resentment or pride to allow others to teach them." She paused again. "The real job of the teacher is to bring students to their own beginning."

"Where is that?" I asked.

"Everyone's beginning is always right here, right now. The doorway to everywhere is right here. The journey always begins when you place one foot in front of the other...and where can you do that but right here?" Once again I was reminded that the most profound truths are often the most simple.

Prema nodded as she saw I understood. "When we can get grounded in the present moment, know our own intention, and remember to always have a question, we have access to everything we need."

I spent the days following our last lesson turning my endless internal comments about life into questions. I tried to establish a dialogue with the Universe rather than running my usual mental soliloquy. I felt insincere though, because I really didn't believe I'd get answers. Thinking about my perpetual indecisiveness and how arbitrary everything seemed, I certainly didn't believe the Universe considered my little life important enough to want a say-so in it.

But wanting to tell Prema that I tried, I made a concerted effort. Perhaps I went a bit overboard. I asked about everything—from what should I do next, to should I choose chocolate or mint chip ice cream? I asked and waited, hoping to hear even the quietest whisper of an answer.

I found that when I did have a real question and could ask it clearly in a yes or no framework, I would get an answer. Somewhere along the way, I realized that the answers were not the main purpose of having a question. I came to see that the question itself put me in the proper position to receive life as it happens. I gained a glimmer of understanding that we live in a responsive universe and that everything we do or think matters. The question then became, "How can I be of service?"

After completing our opening ritual and warm-ups, Prema told the four of us to relax while she spoke to us. "This dance that people call bellydance is made up of four main elements that evolved over vast periods of time and in far-reaching geographical regions. You each began your training with the earliest, the Temple Dance from ancient Egypt. These isolation movements were used in the inner circles of the temples. Some people believe that the priestesses danced for the pleasure of the gods and goddesses. They may have, yet that was only an outer manifestation of their true work."

The four of us sat on the floor listening to Prema. Felicia and Emily sat to her right, and Rachel and I to her left. We were always enthusiastic to hear about the deeper purpose of the dance and the history of the Temple Dance lineage. Surrounded by all the sculptures of the gods and goddesses, Prema's descriptions came to life.

"As you know, a priestess's real esoteric work is about transforming herself into a vessel. Her studies and practices prepare a sanctuary within her to hold the union between Heaven and Earth."

"What union, what do you mean?" Rachel broke in.

"It's a metaphor," Prema answered. "From this union of Heaven and Earth, a child is conceived; this child is Wisdom and Love."

"I'm confused," Rachel murmured. Though I thought I understood what Prema was saying, I remembered to stay alert and watch how others learn.

Pressing her palms together, Prema explained further, "Remember, the priestesses were the leaders and healers of their people. They practiced their rituals to invoke wisdom and to embody love and compassion. In service to their community they sacrificed their personal lives to stay in the temple and open themselves to higher frequency healing energies."

Rachel was still shaking her head.

"It might help to consider an example you're more familiar with—the story of Christ. Most people think of the Bible as a historical account rather than as a map of possibility for individual transformation. Christ represented that potential for all people who followed the teachings. By opening to the Spirit and leading a life of sacrifice, the priestesses became beacons of light for humanity. Like Jesus, they became vehicles for Love and Wisdom.

"There has always been a mystical elite that sought the true and inner meanings of the scriptures. You are coming in contact now with such knowledge." I could almost see a light come on in Rachel's mind.

"If you go back far enough the bellydance has a true mystical lineage. Many will tell you it's a birthing dance, and some of the movements were, and still are, used in this way. But all dance forms evolved from rituals originally created to call upon the gods and goddesses and evoke a spiritual or transcendent experience.

"The remnants of these rituals are evident in many of the world's dances. Think of the dances of India, Africa, Hawaii, Bali, Persia, Brazil, Cuba," she enumerated. "Look at yoga and tai chi—movement forms with the same intention. Some, or all of these forms that I mention, are very possibly direct descendents of Egyptian Temple Dance. More and more historians are coming to believe that the Egyptian civilization is even older than once thought, and that it may well be the mother of all others."

Prema suggested that we get up and stretch a bit. When we settled again, she continued. "When the priestesses were thrown out of the temples and their rituals banned, they continued their practices but clothed them in ways acceptable, or should I say undetectable, to those in power. In this way they safeguarded the continuation of their religion. The dance evolved into an entertainment and was mixed with other rituals to eventually create bellydance as we know it today."

"Why were the priestesses thrown out of the temples?" I asked.

"Ah, good question," Prema responded.

With rapt attention, we gathered closer around her.

"Worship of the Goddess is humanity's original religion, and it has persisted until relatively recent times. The rise of Christianity marked the descent of the Goddess religion. In their contempt for women's knowledge and their desire to create a male hierarchy, powerful men in the early Christian church systematically eradicated the original religion. They defamed the goddesses, banished the priestesses, and destroyed the temples.

"Persecution of this kind continued throughout the Crusades when so-called witches were burned at the stake. These women were teachers, healers, mystics, and even midwives, but the church leaders felt they posed a threat to male supremacy. In another place and time a group of women like us, meeting and studying these unusual practices, would be risking their lives. Of course religious intolerance continues just as strongly these days." With a deep sigh Prema slumped back in her chair as if crushed by the very thought. The room was quiet as we contemplated the ignorance of mankind.

Shaking her head several times as if she just couldn't fathom how such things could happen, Prema sighed again, sat up straight, and moved on. "So, back to the four elements of bellydance as we know it now. Besides the slow isolation movements that evolved from the Temple Dance, the arms play an integral part and have a few different functions in the dance.

"The most basic is to frame the movements." She rose from her chair to demonstrate as she spoke. "Remember, we're trying to focus our energy and put all of our attention into a particular part of the body and a particular energy center. Also, since this is primarily a dance of the torso and our movements may be very small and compact, it's helpful to frame them to show the audience where to look.

"Another function is to speak with the hands, to gesture as they do in Hawaiian hula and the Bharata Natyam, the Indian temple dance. We can tell a story or impart information by signing.

"For an Egyptian Temple Dancer, the most important use of her hands and arms is to move energy around. The isolations and undulations circulate the energy in our torsos as we dance, but the arms extend beyond, directing energy into and out of the body." Prema gestured—beckoning, offering, reaching, holding, and flicking away.

"When we generate and transform energy in our bodies, we need to be able to send it out or summon it in with different qualities. Like tai chi practitioners, we shape and direct energy.

And as in yoga, we make *asanas*—or body postures, and *mudras*—hand postures. Every different posture creates a different quality in the psyche."

"What do you mean?" Rachel asked.

"We all know that on a general level different kinds of movements evoke different states of mind. Change our body…and we change our mind. That's why we like to dance and to make love. Felicitas Goodman, the anthropologist, is doing fascinating research documenting the experiences that initiates of ancient traditions were well aware of. The initiates knew of the transforming power of particular postures, gestures, and movements, and they based their rituals and practices around this knowledge. But these experiments show something even more definitive and fascinating.

"Dr. Goodman noticed that ancient sculptures and paintings from far flung regions of the world all depicted figures in similar postures. Assuming these postures themselves, she and her students found that each one created a predictable and similar experience in all who did them. They weren't just states of mind, but journeys to different interior realms. Some of these ritual postures even created the ability to accomplish tasks in the everyday world."

"Like what?" Rachel asked.

"Well, there were postures for healing, both physical and psychological. And there were postures for divination."

Listening to Prema speak, we were spellbound and impatient to try the postures for ourselves, but she said we'd had enough for one night and sent us on our way. "This will give you something to contemplate in the coming days. We'll continue with the other two main elements of the dance next time," she promised. She held the door for us as we reluctantly left.

While driving out to the East End, I made wrist circles and hand undulations out the car window. After the last class, I'd spent most of my practice time trying to be conscious of my arms, watching in my full-length mirrors to determine the best place to hold them as frames. I created stories as I danced and gestured like a mime. Standing in the center of my living room and sweeping my arms about, I imagined that I was transforming weather patterns around the world.

I was most interested, though, in Goodman's research on ritual postures. The more I heard about the body as a doorway to alternate and ecstatic states of reality, the more I wanted to hear. Arriving for my private class, I tossed my purse behind a chair then turned to ask Prema to tell me more. But she was already beginning our opening ritual.

When we got to the arm and hand movements, she reminded me over and over not to forget the movement's point of origin. "Out of the back—coming from the invisible world into the visible," she repeated. When she placed her hands on the muscles around my shoulder blades, I experienced a searing heat and felt that she was physically branding this law into my body. Forever after that, whenever I touched or moved that part of my body, I remembered the knowledge that she embedded there, planted like a seed.

I felt my body literally becoming a storehouse of wisdom. Or should I say, it always was, but now I was learning where each volume in the library of my body was stored. Beginning the ritual movement each time was like reopening a scripture— the sacred knowledge, like a chant, echoed throughout my being.

Prema tapped me on my lower back. "The energy is shaped from the center," she emphasized, "up through the large muscles in the back. As it comes down the arm, through the hands, then into the fingers, it gets more and more refined." With her hand, she traced the line of energy over my body. "All movements must travel from the most dense to the most refined part of the body. Moving your arm from the shoulder socket doesn't have the strength and integrity that moving from the center has."

I watched as she demonstrated how every part of the body, and the body as a whole, comes in three's. "Look," she said pointing, "the legs, the torso, the head. The upper arm, the forearm, the hand. Even the fingers have three parts. We need to run the energy from our center, in turn, through each and every part, or the movements won't fulfill their potential. As dancers and healers, we want to make sure that the energy reaches its objective.

"Also, our bodies function like batteries. There's a positive and negative current running down opposite sides of the body." Prema placed her palms together at chest level and told me to do the same. "When we bring our hands together in this *namaste* position, we join the two opposing currents. It unifies and balances them and generates a higher frequency. Can you feel your palms tingling?"

I did, almost immediately. "I never thought about why people put their hands together to pray," I mused. Imitating Prema, I moved my hands apart and together a few times, intensifying the feeling.

"Always look for the inner meaning of whatever you see and hear and do. The manifest world veils what's really happening on an energetic or causal level. And the most basic cause is thought—our mind. As I've said before, *energy follows thought* is one of the key laws of the Universe. What you think *will* manifest in the physical world."

I watched again as Prema gestured with her arms and hands. She had such grace, power, and intention in her movements. I felt sure she was communicating something very special though I didn't know the words. "With our arms and our thoughts we reach out to the world. You can see how important it is that we be conscious of what we do with both." Placing her palms together, her body became a prayer.

Enthusiastic to continue where we'd left off last time, our Wednesday night group of aspiring Temple Dancers gathered at the studio.

"Another of the four main elements of bellydance is steps—done in place or traveling," Prema began. "The steps a dancer uses are mostly taken from the folkloric or social dances of her homeland. Egyptian dancers do many step-hip variations." She showed several—her hips thrusting to the side, front, or pivoting. Each movement set the red fringe from her hip scarf flipping in a different direction.

"And Turkish dancers make a lot of their steps hoppy and bouncy like the Karshilama, their national folk dance." Again she demonstrated. "And they're very sexy," she said, doing cutesy shoulder snaps while making pouty lips and flirty eyes. Rolling her head, she let her curly red hair drop over her fluttering lids then brushed it away seductively. We were all a little shocked to see Prema being provocative; she was usually so elegant and refined.

"You'll see Greek dancers doing many variations of the grapevine," she said, traveling around the room crossing front, side, back, side. They're also all over the place, arms and legs wildly going at the same time." Prema's Greek interpretation made us laugh. I hoped she was exaggerating as she twisted, shimmied, and flailed her arms about all at once.

"Of course with all of the current cross-cultural influences, these national and regional steps are now interspersed with those borrowed from many other countries and forms. You see traces of other ethnic dances as well as ballet, jazz and even breakdancing." She gave us another rendition of the Greek dancers, adding a bit of hip hop, sending us into a fit of giggles.

When we finally settled down, Prema continued. "What is the fourth main element of bellydance? So far we have slow isolation movements, arm movements, and the steps. What are we missing?" she asked.

"The hips," we all answered in unison.

"Right," she said. "Where do you think that came from?"

"African dance?" Rochelle asked.

Prema nodded, "The hip movements, accents, and shimmies are influenced by the trance dances of several cultures. We see elements from the *Zar* dances of the Sudan and Ethiopia. The *Guedra* is danced by the Berbers in Morocco; and the Saudi Arabian women's dance is called *Khaligi*. These are all ritual trance dances. Bellydancers use movements from all of these forms.

"So there we have it," Prema said lacing her fingers together. "As it's performed these days, the bellydance is composed of four main elements: isolation movements, arm movements, steps in place or traveling, and hip and torso accents and shimmies."

Though I knew I'd just touched the surface of each, I was thrilled to find that I'd already been introduced to the essential parts of this vast and complex study. Little by little this age-old art was beginning to take shape in my mind and in my body.

When I arrived at class the open and receptive faces of the other women struck me once again. Their enthusiasm was tangible as they attentively awaited the inspiring stories and pearls of wisdom that sprung from our teacher's lips. I took my place and Prema began. "The four main elements of the dance allow us to express the music, whether played by a three piece folkloric band or a thirty piece orchestra. Obviously the staccato and accent movements express the drum and rhythm instruments, but what type of instrument is reflected by the arms?"

"A flute?" Emily ventured. We all turned at the same time to look at her. She rarely spoke and always seemed unsure of herself.

"Why do you say that?" Prema questioned.

"Because a flute is very light and airy and the arms move around softly in the air," Emily answered, sounding pretty sure of herself.

"Exactly," Prema nodded. "A flute is a wind instrument played with the breath. It has that light, lyrical, yearning quality that makes the arms want to reach out.

"To determine what part of your body responds to a particular instrument, you can also look at where that instrument is held while playing. The wind instruments are played at the mouth. They project out and away from the body, as do the arms." Prema held an imaginary flute to her lips, then letting her arms float up, she plucked something out of the air and drew it back down to her heart.

She stood quietly for a moment then said softly, "The flute beckons and evokes the Spirit. In Arabic the word for breath and wind and spirit are the same...*ruh*." She pronounced the word with that breathy guttural sound that makes spoken Arabic sound so sensual.

"So what about the isolations and undulations? What instruments do they respond to?" Prema asked, raising her eyebrows.

Again Emily took a chance, "A violin or string instrument."

"Right again," Prema praised her. "Even in ancient Egypt, a group of musicians would have a drum, a reed flute called a *nay*, and a *rababa*—which is made from a gourd with a long narrow neck attached. The musician holds it upright in his lap and draws a bow across the single string.

"This ancient instrument and its descendant, the violin, awaken a response in the torso and summon the curvy, sensuous isolation and undulating movements. Think of where these instruments are held on the body and notice how the shape of the violin is like the female torso." With both hands Prema traced down her sides as she made slow intense figure eights with her hips and chest. I could almost hear the draw of a bow across the strings of her body.

"The *oud* is pear shaped, very plump and pregnant. The musician holds it close to her womb or tummy. When the strings are plucked, the sound makes your belly tremble." Holding an invisible oud, Prema shimmied lightly, her torso quivering. "All of these instruments tug at the heartstrings and evoke passionate emotions.

"Of course there are exceptions to all my generalizations. Any part of the body can respond to any instrument. Come, get up now and discover for yourself." The four of us jumped to our feet, ready to experiment.

Prema played long recordings of individual instruments. She told us to face away from the mirror, close our eyes and *feel* the music rather than try to make it *look* a certain way. I actually experienced each instrument hitting me in the part of my body that she said it would.

When Prema played pieces that moved back and forth between two instruments, I felt the different parts of my body come to life. I wasn't thinking about what move to make; the sound was moving me. It was as if I couldn't help but respond in that way. Being in direct relationship with the music, I reacted like a marionette with a puppeteer pulling my strings. The spontaneity was exhilarating.

Immersed in listening and responding to the music, I jumped when Prema whispered in my ear. "I knew you'd love this. I can see that your body is highly attuned to the different instruments. You're going to love learning to improvise to the more intricate classical and modern Egyptian compositions."

We spent a long time dancing to music in which each instrument was clearly defined. Then Prema surprised us with a composition that had all the instruments playing at once. We stopped, confused.

"What are you going to do now?" she laughed. "Remember, as a bellydancer you're a visual expression of the music. You interpret what you hear and show the audience what those sounds look like visually. You're saying, 'Look, do you hear that drum beat? Oh, listen to that violin. Ahh…this is what the flute feels like!' But what if it's not clear which instrument is speaking to you?"

None of us answered. "Well," Prema said, "I've found over time that when all the instruments play in unison, they play rather fast as if they're excited to be together. I can always dance to the drumbeat and let the other instruments just swirl around me. No one could fault me for that as long as I stay on rhythm. But there are more interesting ways to reflect the sound. My body seems to respond in three different ways."

I leaned in, not wanting to miss a word. I felt that Prema was about to reveal more precious secrets.

"When I can't hear a specific instrument clearly, I allow myself to be caught up in the music, and I do one of three things. I travel...I spin...or I shimmy until a single sound beckons me."

"How do you know which to do?" I asked.

"The quality of the music tells me. It might push me out of my space, and I'll find myself traveling around the room. Or it will start swirling me into a spin. Or sometimes it creates a vibration in me that turns into a shimmy."

She stopped and looked at our unconvinced expressions. "Why are you so surprised? This is the point of all your studies with me. You're working to become exquisitely sensitive and responsive to what's happening around you. Everything has its own vibration and wishes to be recognized. Each instrument has it's own life and sound which you can reflect back to it. Have an intimate dialogue with the flute or violin or drum, it will teach you what it knows."

We spent the rest of the evening listening and responding to the music. I reveled in the tales each instrument had to tell. I hung on every note, waiting for the story to unfold.

Nights like that were the reason why I found studying with Prema so exciting. Her classes were all a process of discovery— of learning for ourselves—not just believing or adopting what we were told. They were a living experience.

I'd spent the week between our next group class listening to cuts of individual instruments. The rababa, nay, oud, and dumbec each told me their stories, and I responded with my body. I began to feel that each instrument was the guardian of a particular range of emotions. I was learning directly from the music about love and desire, passion and yearning, sadness and hope. The music itself was becoming my teacher. Now, while driving to class, I was hoping that Prema would focus on this subject again and elaborate.

As soon as the four of us were ready, Prema began. "Last time we explored the type of movement each instrument summons from our bodies. We also talked about the four main elements that make up the bellydance as we see it performed these days. Tonight I want you to see that you already have a large working vocabulary of steps that can be used to express the different rhythms.

"There are really just a certain number of steps, and the rest are variations on them. Don't be fooled by the embellishments on a step, learn to read the essence of the movement. You may be looking at a *step hip* or a *hip snap*, but when it's overlaid with a shimmy or different arms, you think it's a step you've never seen before.

"I want you to be empowered by your dance experience. I don't want you to feel there's so much that you'll never get it. Get past the feeling that it will take years before you can really dance. The point is to use the technique as a vehicle for self-expression and as a manifestation of the Spirit. It's not about acquiring more and more steps," Prema said with emphasis.

"Some dancers think you can only do certain steps in a veil dance and certain steps in the slow *taxim* section, but the truth is, you can use any step in any part of the dance. If you understand its essence, you can vary it to reflect the rhythm and speed and instrument you are dancing to.

"This applies to life as well. Look for the essence of what's happening. Don't be fooled by the endless variations of manifestation, which the Chinese call *the ten thousand things.* Remember, our work here is learning to be still inside so we can hear our intuition. Don't be swayed from your intention by the ten thousand distractions."

Prema told us each to make a short sequence with our six favorite steps. She showed us how to vary them by changing the dynamics—size, intensity, level, direction, and floor patterns. Using only those steps, we spent the evening transposing them to various rhythms. We danced to a bouncy Egyptian *beledi* rhythm. We smoothed them off to a slow and slinky Turkish *chiftitelli*, then rocked and twisted the movements to an earthy *Saidi* rhythm. Weaving the same steps together with our veils, we swirled to a lovely lilting *bolero*.

Seeing the variety that was possible with so few steps, I was thrilled that I actually knew much more than I'd thought. Knowing that I could learn directly from the music and use the different dynamics to enhance my limited vocabulary, made me feel like I could take on the world.

Felicia, Rachel, Emily and I were abuzz as we danced down the driveway to our cars. "Don't get trapped in the *ten thousand things,"* Prema called after us.

CHAPTER 8:
MESSENGER OF BEAUTY

P rema and I were driving in her old red Toyota over Lake Casitas Pass on our way from Ojai to Santa Barbara. The long arms of the lake threaded their way through low mountains dotted with rugged California oaks. Avocado orchards blanketed the slopes, climbing up and down steep ravines.

This was to become our Monday night ritual. Prema had decided it was time for me to join the public class she held at the Santa Barbara Community Center. "These students come in response to the class brochure distributed throughout the city," she said in answer to my curiosity. "They're a real cross-section of humanity—all ages and levels of dance experience— all focusing on the same material. You'll have the opportunity to observe a more diverse group and watch how they learn and how the different levels work together."

After hibernating in sleepy Ojai for so long, it was a shock to come into the bustle of downtown Santa Barbara. We parked and went into the community center building.

I'd never seen Prema outside of her almost hermit-like existence. She'd once mentioned that she rarely left her house and knew very few people in the valley. But here, as soon as we entered the building, people rushed up to her like long lost relatives. Many hugged her while she bantered and told jokes, greeting everyone warmly. It was hard for me to reconcile the serious person I saw in Ojai with this effortlessly charismatic social being here in Santa Barbara.

We entered the large mirrored dance room with its shiny wooden floor. Women of all ages, shapes, and sizes began filtering in after us. I was surprised to even see a few men.

The room buzzed with activity. I stretched out and tried to center myself while the other students greeted each other, gossiped, and changed into their dance clothes. Some dressed in leotards and tights, several wore harem pants, while others put on long full skirts. They all had something tied around their hips—chains of coins, simple fringe-edged scarves, or elaborate beaded belts. I tried not to get lost in the glitter and dazzle, but I felt like a kitten trying to ignore the catnip-filled toys in front of me.

As Prema took her place in front of the mirror, the students quieted down. With one look from her penetrating eyes, those who were talking stopped mid-sentence. Stragglers at the door hurried to find their places on the floor. Class began.

We followed a ritual similar to our Ojai class, but there was very little talk or explanation. We kept moving and really broke a sweat. Then we traveled across the floor doing a variety of steps and sequences. Crossing the long diagonal in single file, I felt like I was flying.

Waiting for the rest of the line to finish each traverse, I studied the different types and levels of dancers. They were all doing the same steps, but on each person they looked completely different. Playing their zils as they traveled, the intermediate students executed the movements more or less adequately. Some of the beginners shuffled and stumbled while gazing at the floor, prompting Prema to shout, "There's nothing on the floor. Head and eyes up. Focus in front of you."

But there were a few I couldn't take my eyes off of. I studied them, trying to understand what they were doing or what they possessed that the others didn't. It wasn't that they had more beautiful bodies or prettier faces. And it wasn't the way they dressed; some wore plain leotards with simple scarves tied around their hips.

Observing more closely, I saw that they did the same steps but crisply and cleanly. Though their movements weren't larger, I could really see each step and how it was distinct from the next. Presenting each movement as if it was of ultimate importance, they articulated every nuance. Watching them was like viewing a foreign movie with subtitles stating, "read my hips."

One petite rather plump woman was riveting. She glided across the floor looking majestic. Holding her upper body still, with her head perched gracefully on her neck, her movements were natural, effortless, as if she was born to them. But there was something more.

I realized that the key difference was the aliveness of her face. Her expression changed with each movement as emotions played across her features. Her eyes focused in various directions, and sometimes she glanced down over her cheekbones to indicate a movement of the hip or shoulder. Immersed in the music and allowing herself to fully feel and relish the movements, she let me feel them too. Watching her consciously use the tools of her art, I experienced her dance as a language of direct nonverbal communication.

Once again I realized how hard it was going to be to become a beautiful and accomplished dancer. But seeing her level of artistry inspired me. I began to understand more deeply the consequences of setting my intention and how challenging it would be to stay on track.

The class continued, but I was just going through the motions. I was deep in thought about what I was learning. Following Prema through a veil sequence, I kept catching the silk around my head. While I was blaming my clumsiness on the djinn, she came by and whispered, "Stay in the moment." I began explaining that I didn't want to forget my insights, but she interrupted me saying, "Stay awake!" then turned to critique the others.

Class ended. I waited impatiently as students thanked Prema or requested a private moment with her. I couldn't wait until we were alone so I could tell her what I'd learned. Helping Prema gather her things, I began telling her my thoughts, but she held up her hand for silence and mouthed, "Later."

We walked out to a night fragrant with the scent of jasmine. As we drove away I noticed the sharp crescent moon, like a sickle, hanging above the skyline. We headed down the freeway but instead of turning toward Casitas Pass and Ojai, we continued south.

A few minutes later we turned off the road to the small beach town of Carpenteria. Pulling into the parking lot of a brightly lit supermarket, Prema finally broke the silence. "Each week after class I do my grocery shopping here. The prices are better than in Ojai but more importantly, I need to walk and stretch my legs to stop them from cramping."

The harsh fluorescent lights and crowded shelves of merchandise were a sharp contrast to the elevated empty space of the dance studio. Following her up and down the aisles, I again began telling Prema about my insights, but she handed me her shopping cart, saying, "Practice your 3/4 shimmies."

"Here?" I looked around the empty aisle.

"Dance!" she said emphatically.

Holding onto the bar of the cart, I began. Right hip down-up-down. Left hip down-up-down. The cart steadied my usually wobbly 3/4 shimmy, and the long straightaway was actually a good place to practice. Feeling like a fool, I got to the end of the aisle and prayed I wouldn't meet anyone around the corner. This was definitely not usual supermarket behavior.

Up and down the aisles we went, Prema loading groceries into the cart and me beating out a rhythm with my hips. Forgetting how silly I looked, I really began to get into it. Up on my toes, down on the flats, *tekka dum, tekka dum.* Past the spices and toilet paper, *tekka dum, tekka dum.* Past the Wheaties and peanut butter, *tekka dum, tekka dum.*

By the time we got to the produce aisle I was really feeling it. Remembering what I'd just learned in class about presentation, I articulated my shimmies for the broccoli and tomatoes. I glanced down at my hips so the eggplant would know where to focus. I added a fancy twist to my step for the poor little cauliflowers. Stuck on a shelf, like wallflowers at a dance, their pretty white heads looked so bored.

I stopped short as I rounded the next bend. Glancing up from the dairy case, an elderly couple eyed me. Prema swatted me on the rear to continue and so, under the glaring fluorescent lights, I gave my first real performance. As I danced past them, the couple applauded but then stepped back, perhaps thinking I was contagious.

At the checkout counter the checker and the bagger, the only employees left at that late hour, lit up at the sight of Prema. She bantered with them, asked about their families, told a funny joke, and generally lifted their spirits. "See you next week," they smiled and called after us as we left.

Prema walked regally to the car while I carried her groceries. "It's important to make people feel recognized. In jobs like theirs, they're often treated like a part of the cash register. We're so fortunate to have a practice that inspires us. It gives us plenty of extra energy to spread our light around."

As I placed the groceries in the trunk, I realized that Prema reminded me of a chameleon. Different in every situation, she became whatever was necessary to bring the energy to a higher level. With a small gesture or word, she transformed the environment and left the space in a more positive light.

In the car again, I tried to tell her about my observations, but she shushed me saying, "Don't blow all that energy away by talking. Let it settle now...we'll talk tomorrow."

Frustrated in my attempts to talk to Prema, I could feel the energy roaring through my body. As we sped down the freeway then around the curving road towards home, I could feel the uncomfortable vibrations slowly settle into the silence. By the time we reached Ojai, I had a great feeling of well-being.

We sat in the garden watching Krishna rolling languidly on his back, luxuriating in a ray of sunlight that filtered through the oak tree. I was so excited about our trip to Santa Barbara, I didn't know where to begin. Zealously spilling out my insights about performing and the artistic process, I waxed on and on.

Prema listened patiently, seeming to enjoy my enthusiasm. "You certainly gave a rousing performance in the produce aisle," she laughed. "The cauliflowers were so inspired, I thought they might leap off the shelf and join you." I admitted I couldn't believe she got me to dance since I was absolutely terrified of performing. Then remembering the looks on the faces of the older couple who had caught me in the act, I giggled hysterically. Finally exhausting myself, I asked about the other students.

"The Santa Barbara students come for many different reasons," she explained. "Some just want the physical exercise. Others want to get out of the house for a few hours and socialize with friends. Some are exploring the cultural aspect of the dance. And those who really want to master the dance have a whole variety of goals."

She mentioned a few of the women. One wanted to dance professionally in Middle Eastern clubs and restaurants. One wanted to do bellygrams. Another hoped to dance at her wedding in the spring.

"I noticed that you didn't tell us much about the movements," I remarked.

"With such a range of intentions," Prema explained, "I just keep the class moving and let the music and movement be the teacher. Each student seems to get what she needs, so a lot of talking and explaining isn't necessary. It's a technique class, which is very different than our Ojai class.

"Those of you in the class here are interested in the mystical aspects of the dance and want to teach, so there's a lot of verbal information to impart. And since you're all serious students and committed to practicing, the words are integrated by experience. They're not just more words."

We slipped into a comfortable silence watching Krishna playfully indulge in the pure joy of movement.

∗ ∗ ∗

Our weekly journeys to Santa Barbara intensified my relationship with Prema. I was attending three classes each week. The Santa Barbara class focused on bellydance technique. My private class centered on Temple Dance and spiritual practice. And the small class with Felicia, Rachel, Emily and I integrated the two—the inner and outer dance.

During my private lessons, Prema and I began going on outings together. She always drove. Waiting in her car when I arrived, she'd open the passenger door and say, "Hop in, we're going on a field trip." I looked forward to our excursions and felt like we were playing hooky. She took me to places I'd been before, but with her they took on a completely different significance.

One hot and sunny day—it was always hot and sunny in Ojai—we traveled through the tiny downtown area then turned right off the main road towards Krotona Institute, home of the Theosophical Society. Winding up a long curving driveway through perfectly manicured lawns, we parked next to an old Spanish style building. Prema wanted to do some research in their esoteric library, but first we strolled around the grounds.

Rounding the corner to the rear of the building, we entered a luxuriant garden. Frogs in varying states of development leapt and splashed in the long rectangular pond. Tiny tadpoles wiggled their tails through green algae-tinted water. Others with emerging limbs paddled about, while those with fully developed legs hopped and perched atop the lotus leaves. Transcending their watery beginnings, they lived on land, breathing the same air that we all do. From my studies with Prema, I was beginning to feel like I, too, was transitioning from one world to another.

"Speaking of the breath," Prema said as if picking up a conversation already in process, "just as in life, in dance your breath is your primary partner. It's your first and last relationship in life and also in your dance. You can see who people are by watching how they breathe. Some people breathe very shallowly, afraid to take life in. Trying to stay under the radar, they don't even want to disturb the air around them. Others gulp the air like they can never get enough."

From the moment I began studying with Prema, she constantly reminded me to stay with my breath. "Dance on the breath like a surfer rides the waves," she had taught me. "The movement begins on the inhale and ascends, then finishes on the exhale, like sliding effortlessly down the face of a wave.

Prema stopped walking and watched two frogs vie for the same lily pad. "Your practices will change the quality of your breath which will, like these frogs, allow you to evolve through different realms during this one lifetime." As we walked on, I realized once again that nature reflected the great lessons of life, if I only remembered to look.

Reaching the back door of the library, Prema stopped and put her hand on my arm. "You've become aware on a broad level, that dance is a metaphor for life. But on an individual level, you'll find that the way you dance is the way you live. You'll always know what you have to work on in life by what you find challenging in your dance practice."

Prema continued in a whisper as we entered the building. "You've seen the truth of that with a lot of students. Some find the controlled isolation movements to be effortless but have difficulty letting go and shimmying. While others find the opposite. This applies to even the tiniest of details. Some people have trouble reaching out...so they're very awkward with their arm and hand movements. Others are afraid to take a step or move forward in life...so you see their hesitancy in moving across the floor in class. People's natural personality traits are reflected very clearly in how they dance."

Later, waiting outside while Prema used the library, I pondered her words. I'd thought I wanted to explore the rare old books, but found that I couldn't stay focused on what I was reading. The natural world beckoned.

Sitting and gazing out over the expansive grounds, I fell into a deep silence. I could feel the aspirations of all the seekers who had gathered at Krotona over the decades, searching for wisdom and pursuing their deeper selves. I was beginning to feel a kinship with them.

Thursday afternoon I came ready to dance, but Prema had other plans. She was sitting in her old red Toyota and motioned for me to climb in. I asked where we were going but her response was a quiet, "Shhhhh…"

We drove for over an hour up Highway 33 through Los Padres National Forest until we reached Pine Mountain. The narrow winding road traversed a remote chaparral covered landscape of large boulders interspersed with stark pines. This desolate area is the home of the almost extinct giant California condors. I'd once seen one circling high over Ojai. It was so large I thought it was a plane. With my head out the window, I scanned the sky hoping for another sighting.

We parked at the summit and walked a short distance to a clearing. Prema asked me to sit quietly by myself then strode away, disappearing behind a giant boulder. Left alone in the wilderness, I was spooked. But I was sure Prema was testing me in some way, and I vowed to be prepared.

I breathed deeply, centered myself, and looked around. The silence was palpable; I could hear the bones in my neck creak when I turned my head. Other unidentifiable sounds confirmed I wasn't alone. With each snap and crackle I nearly jumped out of my skin but continued to observe my surroundings.

A long while later, just when I was getting unnerved, Prema reappeared. I acted nonchalant as if we were picnicking in a crowded park, but she wasn't fooled. Sitting on a large rock in front of me, she eyed me closely. I knew that look. Recently she'd been testing me to see whether I stayed conscious when she left me alone.

I remembered everything that happened since she strode off—the color and shape of the leaves on the bushes, the sound of a bee buzzing around my head, the shape of the clouds slowly drifting by, even the trail of ants that marched between the cracks in the rocks.

"So?" she asked with an arch of her eyebrow.

I started reeling off all the things I'd experienced, including the profound thoughts I'd been entertaining.

"Ah," she said softly," but did you allow your self to be seen?"

"What?" I almost shouted.

"Were you aware of the trees and the butterflies and the sun and the plants watching you?" she asked. I was stunned. The thought had never occurred to me.

"Isn't it rather selfish and self-centered to drink in all this beauty and not offer yourself to be seen?"

I just about fell off my rock; I was so taken aback. By now I was no stranger to Prema's unusual ideas, but her question opened up a whole new world. "Please," I begged her, "tell me more."

"Stop thinking for a moment and just listen carefully," she said, leaning forward. "Reversing space is not just an exercise, it's a way of life. Don't be limited to the small slice of life you see through your own eyes. Let life in, pull it into your being, then look through the eyes of everything in and around you. Seeing in this way will expand your limited perception of the cosmos." Experimenting as she spoke, I felt the blinders fall from the sides of my eyes. My peripheral vision expanded, and I could almost see behind me.

Seeing that I understood, Prema reached out and put her hand on my knee. "You must always hold a question and be actively waiting or searching for the answer to be revealed in everything around you. This is a responsive universe, Sherry, stay alert and aware."

I was hanging on every word, so she continued. "Everything is alive and waiting to be recognized. Everything in this world wants to be of service and wants to fulfill its destiny. Life is speaking to you. Learn to listen carefully…everything you need is here in this moment. The next step is right in front of you if you'll only see it and then be willing to take the leap."

Pulling a small portable tape player out of her seemingly bottomless tote bag, Prema handed it to me. "Here," she said, "dance for the trees and the sun and all the little insects."

I watched her walk away, then I put the earphones on and pressed *play*. I felt silly, but I began to let the rhythm enter through my back and make me move. The slow *chiftitelli* rhythm insinuated itself through my body. Soon I was making fluid isolation movements as the energy circulated, tracing a path through my torso.

My arms moved from deep within my back muscles. Then without my direction they began to rise, tracing patterns in the air. I began to feel a connection between my movements and the activity around me. As my hands swept overhead, the billowing clouds seemed to stir then waft in opposite directions as I pulled my palms apart. As I rolled my head, a hawk swept out of nowhere, screeching as he flew away. Until that moment, it had been absolutely quiet, so I sensed he really was acknowledging me.

Absorbed in this elemental play, I found myself moving out of the clearing, gliding in between bushes and trees. I stepped slowly, and every now and then I was compelled to do a figure eight or hip circle. The landscape was filled with patterns, the shapes were already there waiting to be recognized. Catching me in their grip, they pushed my hips or chest into their form. Like flowing along a river, I'd get caught in the eddies and rapids and have no choice but to follow through.

As the music changed to a fast drum solo and reverberated throughout my body, I began to shimmy. Immediately, a couple of bees circled around me, their own tiny bodies keeping time with my vibrations.

As the music slowed, I settled into leisurely undulations. A butterfly landed on my shoulder. I heard a rustling and two deer entered the clearing. We stared at each other. Careful not to startle them with quick gestures, I continued to dance. As they watched me with doe-eyed interest, I felt the sweetness of being recognized.

Is this what we all are wanting and waiting for? I wondered. A flicker in my peripheral vision made me look up in time to see the awesome flight of a condor gliding across the expanse. I knew then that Prema's words were true; the Universe responds to even the smallest thought. Life is truly one vast conversation.

They say that a stone dropped in a still pool ripples out infinitely. I began to see how important it is to be conscious of every thought and movement. I could either send out negative, uninspired energy, or I could transform it through my movements, breath, and thoughts and send out refined and elevating qualities.

I wondered once again what I hoped to bring to the world. If I really could make a change with my thoughts and movements as I danced, what did the world need now?

A slight chill roused me from my contemplation. In the same instant, the deer leapt away and the sun slipped down behind the next ridge. I walked to where we parked the car and found Prema sitting in the driver's seat, eyes closed, and so still I was momentarily afraid she'd passed into the next world.

"Still kickin'," she said as she opened her eyes. "Get in," she laughed, but her eyes spoke of far-distant realms.

Silently tracing the switchbacks down the mountainside, I heard a humming sound echoing all around us. At first I thought it was our tires on the asphalt, but the sounds grew louder and formed into repetitive words, like a Native American chant.

I began to tell Prema what I heard. But before I got the words out, she said, "When we're still, we can sometimes hear the prayers of those who came before us. You know, there really is no time or space. They're just constructs of the mind. This was the sacred ground of the Chumash Indians. They lived and worshiped here for centuries before the Spanish came and killed most of them off."

I wanted to ask more, but she put her finger to her lips and whispered, "Listen."

The whole way down to Ojai the sound of the chanting got louder and clearer, rivaling the intensity of the sunset. The rich voices soothed me. Now and then I thought I saw figures disappearing into the sagebrush alongside the road. The world was becoming more and more mysterious rather than simpler, as I had hoped. Yet at times like this I experienced a great feeling of peace as I gave up my struggle to figure life out. I felt that I *knew* though I still didn't understand.

"You must begin to see as artists see." Prema waited a moment until Felicia, Rachel, Emily and I settled down. "As we dance, we create sculptures with our bodies. What are the things a sculptor looks for in her sculpture?" she probed. "What are the elements she builds into the piece to make it interesting and exciting?"

Looking around, we studied the many sculptures displayed amongst Prema's plants. Because of my art training, I felt I had an unfair advantage, so I didn't answer. Prema waited but the others didn't respond either.

"Form...line...space...these are some of the tools of the visual artist," she said, answering her own question. "People pay to go to museums to see inanimate works of art embodying different qualities and dynamics. Collectors pay astronomical prices to own pieces of art and sculpture. What do they see?" The question hung in the air.

"If we as dancers can make our bodies into interesting sculptures, we've already won part of the battle to hold our audience's attention. By adding a costume to enhance the picture, we captivate them before we even start moving. Then the movement, the dance itself, becomes an embellishment. We can do less and put more into it. This economy of movement gives us time to present every movement consciously and then refine and polish it. You see so many dancers trying to pack too many steps into each phrase or adding unnecessary flourishes that become a distraction.

"Enough words," Prema said, responding to Rachel's quizzical look, "maybe you'll learn by experience.

"Take a place on the floor and begin to move with this new awareness. Take it slowly so you have time to observe. Consider how you look from outside yourself. Create a witness and be aware of the designs you're composing from moment to moment. Look at the shapes. Look at the negative spaces."

Prema played a very slow Turkish chiftitelli and we began moving. Whenever she said, "Freeze," we'd look in the mirror. Then she'd ask if we were happy with the picture we saw or if we'd like to change it. Each time she asked, "Why?" challenging us to contemplate what worked better and not depend on her judgment.

We learned how a subtle twist of the torso creates a more dynamic line instead of having both upper and lower body facing in the same direction. "This is called opposition," she said. "You want to create a dynamic tension and suggest movement even while you're standing still."

We worked on the positive and negative spaces created by moving our bent legs or our elbows away from our bodies. We considered how little details—like the slight tilt of our head, arch of our feet, or articulation of our fingers—changed the whole attitude of the image looking back at us. We saw how holding the same pose, but facing in another direction, produced an entirely unique look. Simple changes added completely new dimensions.

From my past experience building sculptures, this was familiar territory. But using these same concepts on my own moving body deepened my understanding. I felt simultaneously like Michelangelo and his David. Carving away at a block of marble, the sculptor said that he saw the figure living inside and just chiseled away all that wasn't David.

Observing other students grasp these new ideas was vicariously satisfying. I saw them discover the joys of the artistic process, and I stored these lessons away, hoping that some day I'd be able to share these concepts and exercises with my own students.

Eyeing my reflection in the mirror, I struck different poses. I found myself exclaiming aloud, "Oh that's beautiful," or, "Wow, this looks great," or, "How powerful." Then I was saying, "I look great," and "I look powerful." When I heard myself say, "I'm beautiful," I couldn't believe it.

Prema was almost beaming. "How many times have I told you you'd fall in love with yourself one day?" Each time I'd put myself down while looking in the mirror, she'd say, "Mark my words, one day you're going to fall in love with yourself." I had never believed her before, but that day had come. I could feel it beginning to happen; I wasn't fixating on all the negative things I had felt and seen in myself. Instead I was starting to see the beauty I was creating, the work of art I was steadily refining and unveiling through the power of dance.

I arrived inspired to dance and learn more about applying the visual dynamics to my body. Once again things were not as I expected. As Rachel, Felicia, Emily and I filed in, Prema handed each of us a large pad of drawing paper and told us to sit down on the floor.

"Artists do something called gesture drawings," she said, giving each of us a stick of charcoal. "They're very quick sketches made from a live model. They capture the *movement* of the body rather than it's form."

"As you saw in our last lesson," she said, sounding very professorial, "the body at rest can reveal more or less motion depending upon how it's held. We saw that standing straight with upper and lower torso facing forward created a static pose. Then we saw how holding the chest and hips in opposition to each other suggests a dynamism even when you're standing still. We also saw how a slight tilt of the body intensifies the sense of movement even more."

We watched as she twisted her torso then shifted her weight and leaned forward. Each change was a revelation. Prema brought motion and life with each adjustment she made. She was vibrating with energy and vitality.

"For these gesture drawings, I want you to quickly draw the major line of the body to suggest its movement." She put charcoal to paper, and a graceful and dynamic line shot across the pad. One line and a small circle added for the head created a living dancing figure.

I was familiar with gesture drawing from my art training, but the others were delighted to see such simple sketches reveal so much. I renewed my vow to use every bit of time with Prema as the rare learning experience it was. Rather than drift off while she explained things that I already knew, I watched how she taught these concepts.

"Sherry, come pose for us." I took a position while she told the others, "Prepare to draw." She showed them how to hold their charcoal poised above their drawing pads. "Begin," she said. Then almost immediately she said, "Stop!" Felicia, Rachel and Emily had nothing on their papers.

"Quick now, without thinking draw the main line running through Sherry's body." Soon I was rapidly changing poses and they were turning pages just as fast. When we stopped, I was surprised to see how many dynamic looking gestures they had captured. Next Prema asked them to add heads and limbs and hands and feet to clarify the direction of the movement.

Felicia jumped up to pose and I joined the others. As we drew, Prema asked Felicia to be aware of the line she was creating with her body. When she was concentrating, I could actually see the line superimposed over her body. It appeared as a neon-like light glowing through her form. At other moments, she looked out of focus.

"Excellent!" Prema said watching us draw. "Now you're beginning to really see." We continued taking turns, bringing the idea of line and movement into our consciousness from both the inside and outside. "Now put your drawings aside and dance slowly to the violin," she instructed, turning on the music.

Moving in front of the mirror, I could see my own line quite clearly. After a few minutes I also began to feel it. Like a wire armature inside the sculpture of my body, it was distinct and definitive.

Seared into my psyche, this deep integral awareness of my line freed me from needing the mirror. I could *feel* the motion unfolding. Learning to be the artist and the art at the same time made a visceral impression on me. Feeling it in my bones, I knew I wouldn't forget.

I stopped moving to focus on the other dancers. Softening my gaze, I could see their energetic lines even more clearly than their physical bodies. Forms disappeared and I saw luminous, shimmering energy. When the energy turned to colors, I realized I was seeing auras.

I left class feeling like a newborn child.

Walking up the driveway, Felicia, Rachel, Emily and I talked animatedly as we tried to guess what Prema might have up her sleeve for that night. We'd never spoken casually like this before. Normally we'd each arrive separately, come quietly into the studio and prepare for class. Tonight, pulling into the driveway at the same time, we had a few moments to socialize. I wondered as I had when I first met them, who my fellow students were in their everyday lives. Too quickly though, we reached the studio door and stopped our chatter.

"All parts of the visible body come in threes," Prema began after we settled down. "The whole body is made of head, torso, and legs. The torso holds the chest, abdomen, and hips. Look at your arms—you see the upper arm, lower arm, and hand. Your legs have the thigh, calf, and foot. Your hand has the heel, ball and fingers. Your head has mouth, nose and eyes. Even your toes have three parts." We examined our bodies as if we'd never seen them before.

"You need to articulate each part as the energy moves through it. Imagine you're rag dolls and each section of your body comes to life as the energy passes through." We practiced dancing with only our arms—pushing the energy through the shoulder, elbow, and wrist, then drawing it back again. We moved on to the legs, then the torso.

"Oh my, your hands look like dead fishes," Prema exclaimed as she watched me. At first I was offended, but I was to hear these same words many times in my studies with her. I thought I was fulfilling each movement, but Prema pointed out that if my movements didn't come from my center, the energy traveled only as far as the wrist. I remembered seeing fish flopping helplessly as they washed up on the sand, and I knew that wouldn't do. Trying again, I could feel the difference.

Prema gave us exercises to enliven our hands. Putting our palms on the wall, we pushed away with the heel, ball, and then fingers. Then pressing our palms tightly together, we followed through to our fingertips, stretching the muscles open. "Young Balinese dancers do these exercises daily to develop the articulation they need to communicate so expressively. Use everything to bring life to your hands—squeeze your fists, circle you wrists, roll your fingers like a flamenco dancer."

"Sherry," Prema suggested, "try visualizing rainbow colored lights. Imagine each finger is a different colored laser light that beams unbroken to the farthest ends of the Universe. Let each of your hand movements end with these lights sweeping across the cosmos."

Watching her perfectly articulated hands, I could actually see light trails arching across the sky. "So that's where rainbows come from," I laughed.

"Good image," she said, "imagine that rainbows are made by someone dancing consciously somewhere out in the Universe.

Prema's words reminded me once again how sensitive she was to the individual needs of her students. She suggested different ways for each of us to enhance the sense of following through with every gesture.

Felicia was very aural, so Prema had her send out sound communications with her fingers. "Remember how ET wanted to 'phone home'?" she asked. "Imagine you're ET and phone home with every movement of your hands."

Rachel was very tactile. "Reach out and touch someone," Prema told her, "use your fingers to tickle someone on Mars."

Emily was always so withdrawn and seemed to need to do something really big to pull herself out of her shell. Prema told her, "Make your movement causal in a big way—make it earthshaking. When you pass your hand through the air, imagine a tidal wave rising from the sea, or avalanches breaking loose from mountaintops and crashing down the slopes. See it, feel it, create it!"

Waiting outside Prema's house for the others to arrive, I walked around her cactus garden looking at all the shapes and textures. I found my hands gesturing as if I was a conductor and the plants were the instruments in my orchestra. I could hear their sounds, and with my imaginary baton I called forth their songs. I heard laughter and turned to see the other women walking up the driveway, hands in motion, beckoning forces from invisible realms.

I followed them into the studio, and we spent the evening summoning movements from our center. Prema told us to *grow* our arm movements. "Like trees, pull the energy up the trunk from the Earth to the shoulder blade," she instructed. "Push it forward into the shoulder…then like a branch, grow it out to the elbow and down your forearm. Then let your hand unfurl like a new leaf opening to the sun for the first time."

We continued moving as she offered a new image. "Send the energy down your arm as if it's racing down a ski jump. Push it through your dense shoulder blade muscles up into the shoulder. Let it swoop down the arm, past the elbow, down the forearm, and through the bones of the wrist into the heel of the hand. Push that energy all the way through and beyond the finger tips, see it flying off the end of the ski jump into space."

The room expanded as I followed my energy beyond the confines of the walls. The expansive movements felt exhilarating. "Breathe," Prema reminded us, "exhale pushing the energy out into space. Now inhale the energy back into center." The fullness of breath was liberating.

Splitting into two groups, Rachel and I watched while Felicia and Emily danced. They looked like goddesses imbuing each movement with a tangible power. Transcending their human forms, their movements and gestures became archetypal. I believed they could truly be causal, that a sweep of an arm in this room could change the weather on the other side of the globe or heal a broken spirit in a distant land.

It was our turn. Rachel and I began as the others looked on. For some reason I didn't feel shy while being observed. It was as if I had become more than my little ego self who worried about what others thought of me. I felt that I embodied a great power, and it was my duty to share it with the world. My movements were full and alive, and I felt totally present and inspired. When Felicia nodded at me and said, "Good job," I felt like I'd finally arrived.

As we finished, the feeling in the room was rich, unified, and elevated. Looking around our closing circle, Prema smiled with satisfaction. "Very good work tonight...and you're just beginning. You'll learn to extend yourselves to other places in the Universe. Your vision will become clearer, and you will know what's necessary in the moment. You will intuit like a good chef, what ingredients or qualities are needed here. You will know where to find them and how to bring them back."

Always ready for new places and experiences, I was so excited. Prema laughed at my impatience as I coaxed her to tell us more. She only hinted at it. "Remember," she said, *energy follows thought.*"

* * *

Forgetting myself once again, I swung into the driveway, almost running into the others as they walked trance-like around the garden. "Nice of you to join us," was Prema's chilly acknowledgement of my late arrival.

Since I didn't have a clue what they were doing, I watched for a while. Finally, Felicia couldn't resist playing teacher. "We're doing conscious walking," she whispered as she passed me. "Be aware of your heel, ball, and toe as they touch the Earth."

As I began walking I tried to articulate my feet perfectly. It felt very different. Prema had always admonished us to walk like dancers—toe first...gliding into the ball of the foot...and then just lightly letting the heel touch so we'd be poised and ready for the next step.

I moved around the garden—heel, ball, toe, heel, ball, toe. All the while I was trying to figure out the purpose of the exercise so I'd know how to do it right. I was working myself into a thinking frenzy when Prema came up behind me saying quietly, "This is a walking meditation. Concentrate on what you're doing so you can quiet your mind." In my constant desire for approval, I was trying to be the best toe-ball-heeler in history and had once again completely missed the point.

"Now," asked Prema, "can you still be aware of your toe, ball, and heel touching the ground and also stay aware of your breath at the same time? Breathe long, slow, even, and smooth." While the sun went down and turned the sky to a brilliant red orange, we continued silently. Glancing up, I saw the peacock hop onto the stone wall and open his fan.

As if from a great distance, I heard Prema say, "Continue walking and allow your breath to become audible, just a whisper, no voice."

I began to feel fully present, but I felt that I also existed on several planes at once. Observing myself from multiple perspectives at the same time, I was seeing myself through the peacock's eyes, but I was also seeing myself from the top of the century plant.

134   *DOORWAY TO ECSTASY*

peacock's eyes, but I was also seeing myself from the top of the century plant.

I was experiencing what Prema meant when she'd talked about splitting my attention. From the very beginning of my studies with her, she told me to simultaneously be aware of the inside and the outside of the isolation movements. I hadn't really understood why, but now I felt my awareness opening. As my focus expanded, the purpose of those exercises became crystal clear. I was transcending my limited perceptions of space and time.

"Now add voice to your breath," Prema instructed, and soon we were treading lightly and chanting like angels. The garden became a cathedral. The century plant towered above us, and the sprawling California oaks formed a chamber around us. Our voices meshed as we sang soft *ahs* that grew into a resounding *Om.*

Prema quietly broke into our celestial choir, "Continue to be aware of all the previous instructions, and now allow your arms to grow on their own. Don't *make* arm movements, let them happen."

We turned into ethereal creatures gliding reverently through the garden. Our synchronous movements created a feeling of unity—a tangible bond that tightened and loosened as we drew closer or further apart.

Our voices rose to a crescendo then slowly faded into the pervading silence. We continued walking as our arms stopped on their own. Our footsteps got shorter and slower until we were all standing still, our feet anchored to the Earth. Like kelp plants attached to the seabed, our bodies swayed with the ebb and flow of an invisible current.

Prema broke the silence, "Don't talk, hold the energy, and as you go on your individual ways, maintain this deep awareness." I drove home awestruck by the infinite space above me.

* * *

The next day I sat quietly in Prema's garden stringing multicolored glass beads onto a heavy ribbon. I was beading fringe to go on the belt of my first costume. The quarter-inch faceted beads were interspersed with small gold sequins, and each strand ended with a large gold coin. With a long thin beading needle, I made separate strands of graduating lengths. From four inches to eight inches and back again, the pattern emerged.

I struggled to keep my concentration on my work. Every time my mind wandered, I'd string too many beads or forget the sequins or put the same colors next to each other instead of varying them.

Out of the corner of my eye, I noticed the tiny fence lizards doing their pushups while bees hummed along with the tangible Ojai silence. As the sun dappled through the oak leaves, the sparkle of sequins and glint of neon color beads dazzled my vision…

In a flash, I'm shooting into the sky like fireworks on the Fourth of July. Then, falling, falling, with the flickering fading lights, I find myself sitting in a vast open-air chamber. In my lap I feel the weight of a heavy belt of hammered gold that is inlaid with lapis, turquoise, and carnelian. A large scarab, the sacred beetle, symbol of resurrection and immortality, is mounted in the center. Carved from a single stone of royal lapis lazuli, the rich blue gem is surrounded by engraved golden wings. Though they are written in hieroglyphics, I can read the symbols on the metal.

Bright sunlight falls between shadows cast by tall columns. Relaxing in the courtyard leading to the inner sanctum, I enjoy a short respite from my duties as temple priestess. I sit very still, contemplating the words written on the column in front of me: 'Know thyself, and thou shalt know the Universe and God.' *I feel awakened and inspired by these words.*

I look around. The columns and walls are painted in brilliant colors. They feature scenes interspersed with hieroglyphics that depict past Opet Festivals, the most

*important event in Thebes. This year's festival is coming to a
close; it's just moments before the big event. The procession is
making its way down the Avenue of the Sphinxes, the two-mile
stretch from the big temple at Karnak to the Grande Lodge
where I sit waiting. Soon the priests and priestesses will arrive
with our Pharaoh. Today he undergoes the ritual ceremony to
unite with his ka, his divine essence, and be transformed into a
god.*

*I think back over my years in this temple where pharaohs
and high priestesses come to be trained in the Mysteries. Afraid
when I first arrived as a child, now I'm grateful this has been
my destiny. I've delved into hidden knowledge and dwelled in
worlds most people don't know exist, and now I have the
privilege of serving the gods and my people. Hearing a familiar
voice calling me, I rise and anchor the jeweled belt over the
white gauzy fabric that falls softly around my hips. I take a deep
breath, utter a prayer of thanks, and leave to resume my duties.*

A sharp pain roused me from my reverie. I'd stuck my
finger with the long beading needle, and drops of blood spotted
my dance pants. I felt caught between two worlds, not knowing
which self to follow. Krishna, who never paid attention to any
one besides Prema, was licking my foot with his sandpaper
tongue. His cloudy cataract-covered eyes peered intently at me.
As I brought my full attention back into the garden, he meowed,
stretched, and sauntered away.

Prema opened the screen door, setting the wind chimes to
tinkling. I excitedly described my experience. I didn't want to
call it a vision, because I wasn't separate from it. I was totally
immersed in it. I tried to describe my sense of actually being in
the temple and also witnessing the event, but I didn't have the
words to explain.

She nodded knowingly. "Remember, there really is no time
or space," she said. "There really is no separation. Everything is
always going on at once; our minds just perceive events
linearly." She paused to make sure she had my attention. "But
sometimes," she went on, "the veil is lifted, and we see that

what we call the past or the future exists right here with us in the moment."

I asked if that explained déjà vu, precognition, and other so-called psychic abilities or miracles.

"You're always into glamour," Prema remarked sharply, shaking her head. "Some people," she answered, "either through practice or shock or a gift, have the ability to see through the veil. This is what your studies with me will lead you to. Seeing the past in this way is just one of the manifestations of this work."

I leaned forward in my seat. "How can I develop these abilities faster?" My voracious appetite for new experiences reared its head.

"Faster, bigger, better," Prema laughed at me. "Things will come in their own time. They'll unfold naturally with the practices you're already doing."

Seeing how fascinated I was with the idea, she admonished me, "Remember, these are gifts to be used for the good of all. They're not an entertainment, not to be used for your own gain. They carry with them great responsibilities and great burdens. Knowing so much is often far from pleasant."

She saw that in my ever-present desire for excitement, I hadn't gotten what she said. "Oscar Wilde once said, 'There are only two tragedies in life: not getting what you want and getting what you want.' Be careful what you wish for."

She left me there to contemplate as I added one bead after the other, one strand following another, forming my band of fringe.

CHAPTER 9:
LIKE THE WIND

W e wound our way around the undulating curves of the road overlooking the lake. I looked forward to our leisurely drives to Monday night class. We spoke about all kinds of things, and I kept finding that every moment I spent with Prema was a lesson. If I didn't stay present, even while exchanging recipes or talking about painting, I might easily miss some of Prema's wisdom.

After our warm up in Santa Barbara, we lined up in the back corner to travel across the floor. I called this section of class *flying practice.*

"Let the wind be at your back," Prema instructed. "*Zaye al hawa*—like the wind—they say in Arabic."

"This isn't just empty space," she said sweeping her hands through the air. "It's filled with *prana*—the breath of life—and air currents and patterns, and qualities, and everything you need at any moment."

Beckoning to the first person to start moving, Prema animatedly encouraged us as we followed her in a diagonal line across the floor. "Remember there's no separation in this world. We're all sharing the same air, the same breath. Move through it as if you're brushing by your lover, as if you're running toward your soul mate." With each image she made a definitive gesture. We took inspiration from her words and made her actions our own. "Embrace the space. Lend yourself to it. Caress the Earth with your feet. Send your energy down into the Earth to feel her loving support. Slice through the air as if you can feel its substance. Create resistance with the surface of your skin. Then contract your muscles and push through.

"Become a generous dancer. Go out to meet your audience both energetically and physically. Don't make them come to you." Her commands came quickly and emphatically as we flew single file across the room. We shot through the air like birds taking flight. I wouldn't have been surprised to see someone lift off and leave the ground. The power in the room was palpable; I could almost see the air whipping through our hair.

Showing us what she wanted, Prema stepped aside to watch and correct us. She added arm movements to the traveling steps. All the while we played our cymbals *tekka dum, tekka dum*. The energy lifted higher and higher as Prema added turns and level changes. When she instructed us to layer shimmies over all the movements, the room became charged with electricity.

Waiting to cross the floor, I noted our differences in execution. I closely watched how Prema taught by correcting and inspiring each student. I tried to be sensitive to what she expected of each person, but I often didn't understand why she commented on one mistake instead of another.

Later, on our way to the Carpenteria market, I asked her to explain. "By now you see that I'm teaching several levels of technical proficiency, but more importantly, I'm trying to help cultivate more integrated dancers. I've been telling you that the body never lies. With each person, I can see what's happening on other levels. Plus my students tell me things, sometimes very personal things, about what's going on in their lives. In any particular moment, I know there are some things a student just can't hear—critiques that might further weaken her already shaky confidence.

"We're all very sensitive creatures," Prema said, changing lanes. "You know how I always say *you dance as you live*? When you correct or comment on someone's dancing, you're really talking about who they are and how they're choosing to live. People need to know and feel that you respect them when you make suggestions. You also need to know *how* to say it or else they'll feel put down.

"On a very simple level," she continued, "someone may have told me before class that she has a stiff neck or just had minor surgery or even, horribly, that her boyfriend hit her and cracked her rib. For me to badger her about keeping her shoulders down would be not only useless but damaging.

"I had a student once," Prema sighed, shaking her head, "who came back from taking classes in Egypt. Thinking she was suddenly an expert, she kept telling another student to drop her shoulders until the woman broke down and cried. When I confronted this *wannabe teacher*, she said she was just trying to help and accused me of taking sides. I tried to tell her there could only be one teacher in the class, but she didn't understand. She was too full of herself. She left in a huff.

"She continues to dance on her own, doing a nice job of entertaining and creating interesting pieces, but there's no soul in them. They're all about 'Look at me. Aren't I cute and interesting?' Her performances are quickly forgotten."

I was fascinated by how much drama goes on behind the scenes. Busy trying to learn steps and not trip over myself, I hadn't been aware of the interpersonal dynamics.

"It's really a shame," Prema said sadly, "some of the most promising students can't follow through to a higher level. Their insecurities create their drive to master the dance, which makes their performance good technically, and sometimes even emotionally. But it takes years of dancing and living and experiencing to express on a soul level. If they can't hear feedback from someone who cares enough to tell them when their ego is in the way of their spirit, they end up just expressing *pretty but empty*."

Walking into the market, I prayed I'd have the discipline and humility to follow through on this path. Prema shopped while I practiced my step-slides down the long shiny aisles. Gliding through the frozen food department, I could feel the icy wind at my back.

On the drive home to Ojai, I thought about what Prema had told me. Watching people in class, I was already thinking about what they did wrong and what I, if I was their teacher, would do or say to help them improve. Now I realized how presumptuous I was. I had a lot to learn about people before I'd know what, beyond physical technique, they needed. I was grateful that Prema kept reminding me that my dance training was just the vehicle for learning about the bigger picture.

On the way out to the East End, I stopped briefly. The horses grazing in the field on McAndrew Road had captured my imagination as I drove by. I was intently trying to be aware of the Universe speaking to me, and I felt the horses had something to tell me. Getting out of the car, I stood by the fence, waiting for a sign. When nothing came, I remembered Prema telling me, "Let them see you." I tried to empty myself and become transparent so they could sense me. Listening for a message, all I heard was, "You're really late, you're really late," so I hopped back in the car and drove on.

As I opened Prema's door the wind chimes rang like an alarm. "You're late," she said, but her stern expression wasn't half as daunting as the ancient scimitar she held in her hand. Wielding the sword around her body and over her head of flaming red hair, she looked like a wild Viking. "Come here," she said. I thought, fleetingly, that perhaps she had gone mad. But *I must trust* kept running through my mind. *This must be a test.*

I approached cautiously, and she placed the sword on my head, taking a few moments to balance it. "Pull your chin back so your neck is straight and keep your attention on the top of your head where the sword sits." She stood back and observed me. "Now close your eyes and center yourself."

It was hard to compose myself with the sword rocking precariously. "Just keep your attention on the top of your head; this is a meditation on one-pointedness." As I brought all of my awareness to the feeling of metal on my scalp, I felt myself growing taller and the bones of my skeleton dropping down and away from my neck. I became conscious of the straightness of my spine and felt the spaces between my vertebrae. I felt perfectly aligned. Prema had told me many times that perfect alignment allowed the life energy to flow unimpeded along the spine and might open me to other realities.

Concentrating on the free-flowing energy running up and down my back, I dropped into a profound silence. Suddenly my body began to vibrate then shake violently. I thought perhaps we were having one of our California earthquakes...

Tears stream down my face. I want to open my eyes but I can't. I'm kneeling on the ground in a town square. Stones dig into my knees and my hands are tied tightly behind my back. The shouting of the people gathered around me rises to a deafening roar.

A man with a sword approaches and stands beside me. He raises his weapon, and the throng of onlookers grows wilder and more unruly. I think I'll explode with fear and sorrow, and then words come into my head: All is not what it seems. All things change, all remains the same. Be still and know.

I become very still. I feel a soft wind lifting my long loose hair around my head and the warmth of a full sun on a late winter afternoon. A rhythm begins pulsing through me. My body starts to slightly sway, soothing my hurts and fears. I remember that I have control over my experience. Drawing my attention up my spine and out the top of my head, I watch peacefully from above as the swordsman fulfills his duty.

My eyes flashed open to find Prema standing in front of me. "Remember," she said sharply, as the sword began to teeter. At that moment I remembered to keep my attention on top of my head where the sword balanced. I simultaneously recalled the whole vision, which imprinted itself in full detail on my conscious mind.

Unnerved by this terrifying experience, I was wondering what it meant when we heard a truck pull into the driveway. "Quick," Prema said, "run out and make sure they don't run over Krishna." I handed her the sword and was out in a flash. The truck rolled to a stop, and a young man stepped down. I was going to warn him about the blind kitty when I saw his face pale. Looking past me, he raised his hands as if to protect himself and started yelling, "Lady, lady I'm just the water meter reader. Please…I'll leave right away."

I looked over my shoulder to see what the commotion was about and found Prema rushing out the door with sword in hand. Everything stopped. We looked at the sword, *got it,* and dissolved into a fit of giggles, which made the poor guy even more scared.

He jumped back into his truck and floored it. Chasing him down the driveway, I tried to assure him his life wasn't in mortal danger, that I was just learning sword dancing.

We went inside to resume the lesson but laughed ourselves sick instead. Forever after, whenever I'd get too serious, Prema would say, "I wonder whatever happened to the poor meter reader."

The sword vision was always on my mind. What did it mean? And for that matter, what were these experiences I was having? Hallucinations? Alternate realities? Memories of previous lives? By this time, I'd acquired a history of occurrences outside of ordinary time and space. They always took me by surprise. I couldn't make them happen, and once I was in them I couldn't make them stop. I didn't know if they were telling me something about my present life or reminding me of some distant past.

Whatever they were, I was learning important life lessons. Whenever I came out of them, I felt I'd been handed another law for leading a life of intention. *All things change, all things remain the same. Be still and know.* These powerful words had shielded my true self as my body was destroyed in such a violent and horrifying manner. Somehow I'd learned to stay conscious and lift my awareness from my emotional center to a place of witnessing. *What irony,* I thought, *I didn't lose my head when I was actually about to lose my head.*

When I asked Prema about these bizarre events, she told me not to label them or compare them to anything I was familiar with. Instead, I should contemplate them and keep them alive as real experiences. All she would say definitively was, "Remember the Mystery. Life is so much bigger than you think." I wondered if I would ever understand.

INITIATION III:

THE WAY OF PERFORMING

CHAPTER 10:
STALKING THE MASTER DANCER

I dawdled my way up Prema's driveway. Opening the studio door, I felt a mixture of excitement and trepidation. Prema had decided that I needed to begin performing, that it was the next step in my spiritual development as a dancer. She wanted me to be part of the Shakti Dancers, her small troupe. They danced at fairs and festivals, private and public events, and often at senior centers and nursing homes. She explained that Shakti is the Hindu goddess representing the divine feminine creative energy. "I chose that name to give the troupe a very high aspiration."

The thought of performing was both thrilling and terrifying. I was a long time member of that huge group of people whose number one fear is public speaking. If I couldn't feel comfortable talking to an audience, how would I ever feel up to dancing for them as a mere beginner? There was still time to back out, but I didn't know how it would affect my relationship with Prema.

All through class I vacillated, but when it ended I didn't grab my stuff and bolt. From now on I would stay later for rehearsal. I watched Felicia, Rachel and Emily relaxing as they waited. They had all performed together for varying lengths of time. I'd be the fourth person in the troupe, the new kid on the block. A bundle of nerves, I was anything but relaxed.

"Before we begin," Prema looked intently at each of us, "it's important to always remember that we're using the dance as our spiritual practice. For most dancers, the performance is the end goal of their hard work. For us, our classes, rehearsals, and performances are the mirrors we use to focus, clarify, and reflect our state of awareness.

"Keeping that in mind, let's begin to prepare for performance." She searched each of our faces to make sure we understood our shared intention. "You've worked very hard on developing your bodies and refining your technique, and you've learned sequences and choreographies. You've also learned to name your movements as you dance them. This is so important; you can't depend on muscle memory alone. In performance, many different things happen to make you forget your choreography. If you're distracted, if you had problems at home, or if you're thinking of anything else, it will interfere with your dance." Prema was voicing my greatest fear. I was petrified that I'd forget the steps and look like a fool.

"Or," she continued, "the lights may be so bright they're startling, or you see someone in the audience you know or didn't expect to see. Any of these things can make you forget your choreography. And as you've heard, *the show must go on.* So many times in my own performing experience," Prema admitted, "I've been saved by the verbal tape of steps running in my mind, telling me what's next."

Pausing dramatically for a moment, Prema surprised us by suddenly spinning around and striking a pose. "It's show time!" she sang out. I giggled in excitement, releasing my tension. The curtain was about to rise on a new act.

Felicia and Rachel laughed at my nervous enthusiasm. While waiting for me to settle down, Prema reminded them that they couldn't learn anything new if they came to class with full cups. "Remember *beginner's mind*—come to class and to every moment of your life as a beginner." Put in their place, they looked properly humbled.

"Now," Prema went on, "as we practice dancing as a group and projecting our performance to our audience, we will learn to use the dance as a language of communication. We need to connect physically, emotionally, mentally, and spiritually."

We rehearsed a beledi dance she'd been teaching us. "So, now that you know the steps, begin to consider how you're communicating. As you do the dance again, be present and allow yourself to be seen."

She stood right in front of us and watched. I became increasingly uncomfortable thinking about all my shortcomings, both physical and technical.

"Imagine your audience watching you dance. Let it be okay for them to see you as you are now; you don't have to be perfect before you perform. If you wait until then, you might as well forget it. The better you get, the more you'll expect of yourself. Perfection is always just out of reach." I thought about how many endeavors I'd given up on, knowing I'd never be more than mediocre at them.

"Do the dance again and think about performance in a more creative way," Prema suggested. "When I first began performing I had tremendous stage fright. Then I thought about how uninhibited children are and how they're always asking us to watch them do this and that. Allow yourself to be a child and let the audience watch you explore. Imagine you're discovering, for the very first time, how wonderful it feels to dance. Let your audience share that experience."

We repeated the dance. Holding the image of children at play, we loosened up and just enjoyed dancing. We were still focused, but the heaviness in the room had lifted. "Much better," Prema remarked, "you all look more relaxed. Children are spontaneous, joyful, delighted at their own activity. Put that into your dance. Now, once more with feeling.

"Excellent," Prema complimented us as we finished the dance, "now we're getting somewhere. Remember, people love to be entertained; they're wishing they could be up there with you. Typically the ones who are most critical are the ones who would most like to be in your dance shoes. Be a generous performer. Focus on what you want to give, not the acceptance or praise you want from your audience.

"Let's begin again. Visualize the audience and let your dance be your gift to them. Dance as you do in your own living room when you're imagining that you're a great star." We laughed with embarrassment, recognizing our shared fantasy.

"You have to get over yourself," Prema stated passionately. "Shyness is all ego. It's about trying to control how people see you." Her words struck a nerve.

I kept dancing, but my mind was busy with this latest insight. When I used *shy* as an excuse for not acting, was I really saying, "I won't talk to you, or dance for you, because you might not see me the way I want to be seen." Was I keeping myself locked inside a little box sealed with a label of my own making?

"Earth to Sherry," Prema waved at me. I was bumping into the others and turning the wrong way. "You can think later, but right now the show must go on."

We began from the shimmy section and almost immediately Prema stopped the music. "Ladies, this isn't a funeral, you know, you all look so serious. Begin again," she said, demonstrating, "and imagine that this is your party. Greet your guests. Take them around and introduce them to each other. Let them see your new outfit. Make sure they feel welcome. Serve them. Your job is to make them feel comfortable so they can relax with the confidence that they're in the hands of a professional. Then they can sit back and truly be entertained. If they have to worry about you feeling secure enough to perform, they won't be able to enjoy themselves."

We started over. I imagined a large crowd of people watching in delight as I danced. We rehearsed over and over again until my extreme anxiety abated. Still, when Prema said we'd soon dance for each other, my butterflies returned.

"Now we're going to start building new levels of awareness as we rehearse. Can you continue to visualize your audience while also being present on the first beat of every eight count measure?"

We repeated the dance again and again, trying to maintain our three awarenesses at once. Visualizing the audience, verbalizing the choreography, and trying to be present on the first count of every phrase was a full time job. By the end of class we were all dripping with sweat and jittery with the energy we'd generated. As we made our closing circle, we were wide-eyed and giddy with awareness. To integrate and balance our energy, Prema began chanting, "RA MA...RA MA," the Hindu masculine and feminine sounds of the Universe. As we joined in, a serene feeling of harmony descended.

"Our goal as performers," Prema said softly, "is to become increasingly aware of *everything* while we're on stage. Being a Master Dancer is being conscious of what's happening in the entire theater. From the most minute gesture she makes, to an awareness of her breath rising and falling, to the responses of her audience, a Master Dancer is continuously *aware*."

We walked quietly out into the night.

As I drove out to the East End of Ojai, I prayed that this wasn't the night we'd have to dance for each other. While practicing between classes, I held the idea of the Master Dancer before me, but I really couldn't feel what that meant. I could barely even stay aware of the choreography throughout a dance. And when I thought of dancing for my classmates, I promptly forgot my next step.

We all arrived on time and Prema began immediately. "Last time we explored some of the physical aspects of performing. We imagined an audience and let it be okay to be seen. We also worked on being present at the beginning of every phrase. We could explore each of these awarenesses for a lifetime, but right now we have a performance coming up and have so much more to do before then."

Everyone started talking at once, asking when and where.

"Whoa," Prema silenced us.

I was shaking. I'd been warming to the idea of performing, but now that it was becoming a reality I was terrified.

"We've been asked to dance at a gathering in Santa Barbara in six weeks. We have to be ready by then. We have much work to do, and we also need new costumes."

Speaking all at once, we asked about the style and color. Again Prema brought us back, "If you can't perform well, it won't matter what kind of costume you wear, so let's get back to our rehearsal."

Disappearing behind the screen, Prema started the music. The familiar rhythm immediately overshadowed my nerves. I was ready when she came out and said, "Let's dance. Once again, let's build our awareness to include all the things necessary to create a meaningful performance. Remember, our purpose is to really touch our audience and nourish their spirit."

As we took our places on the floor, Prema instructed us, "This first time through visualize your audience, see them clearly in your mind's eye." I'd been practicing, imagining a large crowd in a packed theater. "They're your partners," she reminded us, "you're dancing to come into relationship with them."

Before our second run-through, Prema emphasized, "This time be aware of your breath. Realize that it's flowing back and forth between you and your audience. It invisibly carries your intention and wishes to them. Remember, we all share the same breath. If you hold yours, the audience will also be breathless, but not in a good way," she laughed.

"Now this time can you be aware of being seen, breathe consciously, and also be totally present on the first beat of every phrase?" After several repetitions, I was silently applauding myself for getting it. Then Prema dropped the bomb, "Are you reciting the choreography in your mind?"

At that point I lost it. I couldn't concentrate on anything. Prema could see that we were all struggling, even Felicia and Rachel. "Take a short break then come back ready to continue."

We each took the time to center ourselves. I walked out into the garden and searched the sky for the brightest star. Then standing in the moonlight, I let the silent vast emptiness sweep my mind clear. I walked back in refreshed and ready to begin.

"Let's go on," Prema turned up the music.

Hearing the drum break, we picked up the choreography where we'd left off. "Now, can you feel the line of your body and still hold all the previous awarenesses?" Again, our dancing fell apart.

"Stop for a moment and turn away from the mirror," Prema said, turning down the music. "Can you see in your mind's eye the picture you're making with your body? See yourself from outside. What does your witness see? Move slowly and imagine moving from frame to frame in a motion picture. Notice every detail. Is the line as defined as it can be? Is your posture impeccable?" Standing in one place, I could just about manage everything. But as soon as the music began and we had to dance up to speed, my house of cards collapsed.

Prema didn't stop us this time. "Observe the details. How are you holding your head on top of your neck? Are your hands and fingers alive and expressive? Are your feet beautiful? Are you caressing the Earth with every step?"

We rehearsed our choreographies several times, trying to get a handle on all the subtleties. It was like trying to juggle. Just when I thought I could keep all the balls in the air, Prema threw in one more and everything slipped from my grasp and fell to the floor.

"Focus ladies, concentrate! If you can't maintain your attention while dancing in place, what's going to happen when you have to change floor patterns and move in perfect unison?"

We groaned.

"We have to add extra rehearsal times or we'll never be ready. Be here on Friday evenings at seven."

We finished class in a circle. Dripping wet, we wiped the sweat from our eyes as Prema reminded us that we were now a group—a small tribe dependent on one another. "You must commit yourselves, not only to your own practice but also to each other. You must become one entity, one cohesive unit that moves and breathes together with a shared intention. Join hands," she instructed.

We stood with pinky fingers linked so we could still hold onto our finger cymbals. Prema's all-seeing eyes traveled slowly around the circle. "Don't let your images of each other be a barrier to the flow of energy between you. Let go of your judgments and forgive each other for any shortcomings and trespasses." Shifting from foot to foot, we avoided each other's eyes.

Glancing quickly around the circle, I realized my resistance. I still resented Felicia for trying to tell me what to do. I also hadn't made any effort to get to know Emily because she seemed so reserved. Rachel I liked, but I'd dismissed her as bland and uninteresting. I thought she was a bit of an airhead.

I shook my head vigorously, hoping I could clear my mind. I tried to imagine I didn't know any of them and that we were meeting for the first time. I felt the increased flow of energy around the circle and everything got visibly lighter.

Prema broke into the uncomfortable silence, "Now repeat after me, 'I am a Shakti Dancer. *We* are Shakti Dancers. We ask to be allowed to dance for the healing and joy of all beings.'"

As I repeated the words, I began to feel I was a part of something larger than myself. I fervently hoped I'd be able to overcome my fears and not let the group down.

"What's the shortest route between the dancer and the audience?" Prema asked.

When none of us responded, she told us to contemplate her question until we met again.

Walking to the car, I looked up and saw the stars shining on me like spotlights. Imagining myself center stage on opening night, I danced between thrill and terror.

Afraid I was late, I raced up Prema's driveway, dropping and retrieving my dance gear, stumbling as I ran. Following on Emily's heels, I just caught the door as it was closing behind her. We'd barely put our things down when Prema began. "You must learn to move like a flock of birds or a school of fish.

They move in unison, changing directions and patterns as one being. In all dimensions, they keep an equal distance between themselves. Now how are you going to do that?"

"By watching each other," Emily answered.

"And?" Prema prompted. "Birds and fish also travel in the dark."

I conjured images of geese taking flight and immediately forming perfectly spaced patterns. Then I recalled snorkeling amidst a school of fish. Rapidly darting this way and that, they kept the shape of their group as a whole.

"They must *feel* each other and maintain a certain surface tension between them," I ventured.

"Well put," Prema nodded, "we can do the same thing by extending our energy beyond our physical bodies and sensing each other and the space around us. It's difficult in the beginning, but after awhile it will become second nature to you.

"Up until now," Prema continued, "I taught you the dances as solos, now I'll be able to stage them with more complex and interesting floor patterns." She had us change places by traveling in circles and diagonal lines, switching rows forward and back. She kept re-arranging us in different groupings until she was satisfied.

"Now let's do the dances several times with your focus on *being where you need to be when you need to be there.*"

We stumbled about, plowing into each other in our overzealous race to be in the right place for each sequence. It was a whole new ball game. It didn't even feel like the same dance. We finally got it together when we began to *feel* the patterns we were making as a group.

"Stop and catch your breath," Prema suggested. "Remember that everything you learn as we rehearse extends well beyond the studio door. The lessons of the performance stage are applicable to the larger stage of life. There's a perfect design for every unfolding moment. If you just jump into it without respect for the integrity of that pattern, you'll just create chaos rather than enhance what's already there.

"Knowing where to be and also where not to be is a great life skill. Changing your position even a little can give you a completely different perception of the events happening around you. Then you'll have a better vantage point from which to be effective. And of course I'm not just talking about the dance or the external world; this applies to your inner life as well. Looking at your feelings from a new angle gives you the space to see things in another light and shows you a fresh way to respond."

Prema's observations always opened up my world. Before, I'd been concerned about running into the other dancers. Now I was contemplating the possibility of one day effecting change in the world.

"Let's dance!" Prema called us back to the smaller stage. "Be where you need to be when you need to be there."

Taking our places we began again. Prema reminded us over and over to make straight lines. "Guide right," she told us. "The dancer on the far right sets the line; then you each keep an eye on the person to your right. Remember when you turn around or turn in a different direction, the person on the right may change."

Although it seemed perfect, Prema kept shouting, "Guide right, your lines are awful." Finally she stopped the music. "Do you know why I'm harping on the lines being straight?" she asked.

We shook our heads. "Our minds are always seeking order, but our eyes always go to the thing that's out of place. It's like a piece of dust on an otherwise perfectly clean floor or a chip in your nail polish. You can't keep your eyes off of it. When one of you turns the wrong way or the space between you gets uneven, the viewer's sense of order is disturbed."

"But if we're always watching each other," Rachel asked, "won't it look like we don't know the steps?"

"Good question," Prema nodded. "Actually, you can see a lot from the corner of your eye. But it's also perfectly fine to look at each other and smile or interact on stage. Last time I asked you what the shortest route to the audience is. Have you thought about that?"

None of us replied. "The shortest distance to the audience," Prema paused, "is through another dancer! Think about it. You may not be able to bridge the spatial and emotional gap between you and the audience, but they can certainly see the relationship you have with your fellow dancers. This gives them instant emotional access to what's happening on stage. That's how actors pull the audience in, by relating to other actors on the stage. So by all means, look at each other and share your feelings and at the same time check your lines."

As we continued rehearsing, I tried as hard as I could to stay attentive to all of the things Prema asked of us. I was being introduced to the magic of performance and entrusted with the secret tools of the trade. I wanted to be worthy.

With my private classes, the Santa Barbara class, and the extended rehearsals twice a week in Ojai, I was living and breathing dance. I lapped it up like Krishna at his bowl.

Between classes I spent my time rehearsing on my own. I was amazed to find my usually undisciplined self faithfully keeping my practices going. Even when I just wanted to lay around, I put on the music. Feeling summoned by the Spirit, I was up and dancing.

Prema had told me to always continue the ritual practices, as they were the most important pathway to my spiritual development. The dancing and performing would help me learn to share with others but would be useless if I had nothing of significance to offer. By returning each time to basics, my private classes were devoted to deepening the inner practices. "These basic movements and concepts," Prema reminded me, "hold within them all of the important teachings."

As performance time neared, I grappled with my intense stage fright. Prema kept telling me that it was all ego. She said I was afraid to be seen as I really am; and that I was trying to put up smoke screens and control how others saw me.

"You can't live your life caring about what other people think of you," Prema said matter-of-factly. "No matter what you do, they will think what they choose to. What we see in others is more a reflection of ourselves than of them. But all of this psychological stuff doesn't matter. Your whole practice with me is about learning to live from a deeper intention. You can't solve problems on their own level; you have to transcend them."

"But how do I get over this?"

"I'm not buying this *poor me* stuff," she retorted. "Don't play Sherry *trying* to get over her limitations. Pull yourself out of the abyss of your ordinary reality. Go beyond your narrow vision. Let go of your personal story…be born again as a new being. Turn to the light…don't keep crawling back to the familiar comfort of the known. It's your choice."

As she prodded me, I remembered moments of freedom and beauty and of dwelling in an open unlimited state. But then when I thought of performing, I rapidly deteriorated into a sniveling little wretch, hiding in the shadows.

My life had become one continuous dance class. It seemed I was always showing up on Prema's doorstep. Each time in the moment before I stepped over her threshold, I'd think, *here I am again.* I'd remember how grateful I was to have this dance and this teacher and this studio as a refuge. It was truly an ashram, my place to practice dwelling in the Spirit.

"Why do people leave the comfort of their homes and their regular television programs to come out and see a live performance?" asked Prema as Felicia, Rachel, Emily and I quietly tried to center ourselves.

She immediately answered herself. "They're looking for a different experience of their lives. They're looking for an emotional experience not provided by their habitual schedules and activities. They're looking for a *feeling*, not a technical display."

Prema continued to probe, "What does the audience focus on most while watching a live performance? It may surprise you to know that ninety-five percent of the time—whether it's a play, a musical, a vocal concert, or a dance performance—the audience is watching the performer's face."

She stopped to let her words sink in. "Think about it," she went on, "even if the action is amazing, aren't you always searching the faces of the performers to see how they're feeling about what they are doing?

"A performer learns to pull our heartstrings with her facial expressions. We'll feel what she feels. That's what makes a true performer; she's really in touch with her emotions. She doesn't fake it. She's learned to tap into a deep wellspring of universal feelings. Then with her artistry she creates an emotional world that we totally believe in. That's the magic of performance!

"As we rehearse our dances tonight, I want your focus and intention to be on showing me how the music and movements make you feel. Allow your faces to be fluid and expressive. Let your emotions play on your features like a breeze on a pond. I should see you listening to the music, reacting to it with your facial expressions, then responding with your body."

Prema started the beledi music and we began the first dance. I felt embarrassed as she intently watched our faces for signs of expression. "Stop, Stop! You'd all make great poker players," she exclaimed lowering the music. "I don't see a clue as to how you might be feeling about what you're doing!"

Taking a deep breath, she exhaled with a sigh. "I can see we have to approach this a little differently. Let's warm up our faces just as we warm up our bodies before dancing.

"Turn away from the mirror. Now I want you to make a silent scream. Do you know the painting 'The Scream' by Edvard Munch?" A couple of us nodded. "Make your scream as harrowing as the man in the painting. Even though we can't hear it, we can feel his torment." We tittered in embarrassment as we tried our silent screams.

"Mouths wider," Prema ordered, "your eyes should be popping out of your head." She shook her head, "I don't believe you ladies, find some motivation, what are you screaming about?"

I searched through my mind for something that terrified me. Spiders? Snakes? Violent men with weapons? Being trapped with no way out? That did it. I silently screamed my head off.

"All right, all right," Prema finally said, "now I believe you."

"Now very slowly contract those face muscles and become a little old wrinkled prune-face. That's it," she encouraged us. "More," she said. "Get older...no teeth...sink those lips in." Sneaking a peek at the others, I felt like I was with a bunch of crazy old crones. We all burst out laughing at the same time.

"Good," Prema said as she stopped laughing. "Now find a neutral expression—relaxed but alive."

I was impatient to get back to the dancing, but Prema still wasn't finished with the face stuff.

"Slide your jaw back and forth several times...now slide your tongue side to side and up and down. Now all around...try to lick beyond your lips. Can you touch your nose with your tongue?" We'd gone beyond feeling silly and were really getting into it.

"Wiggle your nose," Prema instructed. "Now flare your nostrils...eyes side to side...up and down...now all around in both directions." We looked like fierce Tibetan demons.

"Now wiggle your ears." We tried, then realized that she was teasing us.

When she finally stopped laughing, Prema applauded our efforts. "Good job," she nodded. "Work with keeping your faces pliable and mobile. Add these exercises to your individual warm-ups."

We began dancing again, but again Prema stopped us. "I don't think you realize how important this is. Get your veils." I thought we were going to start our veil dance, but Prema had other ideas.

"Put your veil over your face…yes…let it cover your face. Now walk slowly around the room." We looked like a bunch of kids playing ghost at Halloween. "When I say a word I want you to stop, lift your veil, and show me the living presence of that emotion on your face. *Become* that emotion.

"Happy," Prema called out. We stopped, lifted our veils and made a face. "Don't *make* faces," she exclaimed, "feel the emotion and allow it to play across your features."

"Try again." A whole gamut of emotions followed—"Sad, confused, sexy, scared, hopeful, shocked…"

Prema quickly called out the feelings, and we rapidly dropped and raised our veils to keep up with her. The speed didn't give us time to think, just to react.

"That's it," she encouraged, "you know how quickly emotions hit us. We feel them before we're even cognizant of them. Let your facial response be immediate. We've become so adept at hiding our reactions, but now you must be willing to share your emotions with your audience and allow them to feel *through* you."

We ran through the dances several times. The wall that usually kept my emotions in check fell in chunks around me, releasing a flood of energy like water through a ruptured levee. I felt washed clean.

I was literally a bundle of emotions when I arrived at Prema's for our Friday night rehearsal. I'd spent the time between classes working on allowing my feelings to show on my face. I sat for hours on my living room floor in front of the mirror. Thinking of an emotion and trying not to *make* the appropriate face, I'd let it well up from inside. Over and over I'd return to neutral then see how quickly I could summon up real feelings. When I realized how much energy I expended trying to hold them in, it was a relief to just let go. Often I'd get caught in one emotion or another, and I'd sit there crying or wailing with anguish, or rolling on the floor in glee.

I was so glad my little cabin wasn't within hearing distance of the neighbors. If I had lived in an apartment, some concerned citizen would surely have called the authorities to haul me off to the loony bin. It was scary to feel so raw and over the edge but also liberating to release so much pent up emotion.

Now as I walked up the driveway, my face danced to an inner passion play. I expressed love for the palm tree, fear of the cacti, sadness for Krishna's sightless existence, and anger at the thorny bougainvillea that caught at my skirt as I brushed too closely by.

As soon as we warmed up, Prema asked us each to choose a section of our favorite dance and perform it for the others. What I feared most had finally come upon me. While waiting for my turn, I was shaking so hard I couldn't concentrate on watching the others. Unable to think of a way out, I chose a part from our veil dance, imagining I could hide behind the silky fabric.

The others finished and Prema called me forward to take a pose. My knees were knocking together so loudly, I feared I wouldn't hear the music. "Okay, right now in this moment, what are you feeling?" Prema asked.

"I'm scared to death," my whispering voice wavered.

"You're having a physical experience, that's obvious, but why label it fear?"

I didn't understand what she was getting at.

"What is your body doing?"

"It's shaking like a leaf."

"It looks like a shimmy to me and a pretty good one at that," she countered.

I looked down, saw my fringe swaying, heard the coins chattering, and my mind stopped. I couldn't remember what was going on.

Just as I realized that I was still standing in front of everyone and was expected to perform, Prema, in a loud commanding voice, yelled, "Stop! Don't think...stay with the movement." She nodded at my vibrating hips. "Could you just call this a shimmy?" she suggested.

Startled, I glanced down and my shimmy started to stall.

"Stay with the movement," she ordered again, "don't listen to your mind telling you useless things."

I tried to stay with the feeling of the shimmy.

Prema saw my mind begin to move and countered, "If you have to label your feeling, why not try calling it *excited*?"

I told myself I was trembling with excitement.

"Now breathe," Prema said. I inhaled and exhaled, concentrating on my shimmy.

"Can you let it be okay for us to watch you shimmy?" Prema gently asked.

I looked into the eyes of the women watching me. As I was about to panic again, Prema intervened. "Watch your mind. You're in a place prior to thought. Choose to replace your fearful thoughts with positive ones. Say, 'I love having people watch me dance.' Say it out loud," Prema ordered.

I opened my mouth, but nothing came out.

"Say it with conviction," Prema prompted. "Say it as if you believe it."

At first the words only emerged as a whisper, then as I repeated them over and over they got louder and clearer.

"Good," Prema said, "now relax."

I exhaled loudly, feeling calm but energized.

Speaking to all of us, she said, "Most all of our fears and problems are a result of defective thinking. Remember, *energy follows thought*. You just saw Sherry caught up in a fearful thought—possessed by it—then she consciously banished it with her attention, breath, movement, and affirmation.

"Are her fears about performing all gone? No, but now she's learning the tools to confront and overcome them. But she has to be vigilant and continuously defend herself against her negative thoughts until they loosen their hold.

"Negative thoughts are just parasites. They're demons. They're the devil. They're decisions or labels you put on past experiences. They're like vampires. They cling to you and feed off of you. Don't nourish them. Do not entertain them. Your tools are weapons to prevent negativity from controlling your life."

I felt like I'd been through a wringer, and the other women seemed a little stunned, as if they'd participated in an exorcism. "And so you have," Prema said when Rachel voiced that thought.

Prema thanked me for facing my fears. "I think we all learned a valuable lesson. If you can handle this, then performing will be a piece of cake. Repeat after me, *performing is a piece of cake.*"

"Performing is a piece of cake," I parroted.

"What did you say?" Prema asked, cupping her hand to her ear.

I laughed, "Performing is a piece of cake!"

Prema began our rehearsal as soon as we warmed up. "We've concentrated on facial expressions as the barometer of emotions. As I mentioned before, the audience watches our faces to get an emotional reading on what's happening and how they should be feeling. Now how else can we increase the emotional intensity of our performance?"

"We could change the way we do our movements," once again shy Emily surprised us by coming forth with an answer.

"Such as?" Prema questioned.

"Well, when we want to express happy, we could make them more bouncy. Or if we're trying to be shy, maybe we can face back and look over our shoulders. Or to be sexy, we can make our movements slow and slinky."

"Very good," Prema praised Emily. "You're talking about changing the dynamics, the tools of a movement artist. Giving movements different dynamics changes the emotional content— we can change their size, or speed, or direction, or level, or intensity."

"What is intensity in movement?" I asked.

"Intensity is the amount of energy you put into your movements. You can deliver a small movement with a real *pow!* Even though it's small, it will pack a punch. Or you can take a very large movement and make it very slow and languid, and it will read as cool and relaxing. Or if it's really, really, really slow," she said, drawing the slowest hip circle in history, "it might say hot, hot, hot!" She added a come hither smile to emphasize her point.

"As you take each step, consider how you want the audience to feel about it. You can tell an ongoing emotional story as your sequence of steps unfolds. Just like a painter considers what color to make each stroke on a canvas, you need to decide how to shade and texture your movements."

We rehearsed our dances over and over. "Speak with your body," Prema kept reminding us. "What are you saying with that shoulder roll? How about that spin, can the audience feel your abandon? How about those arms? Show me how much you're yearning, beckoning, calling.

"If you don't imbue your dance with emotional content, your audience won't care how technically proficient you are," Prema reiterated. "They'll just feel bored." She patted her mouth, yawned, and sighed, "Ho hum. It's like food, if you don't serve your guests, they'll just sit and look at it. They won't know it's okay to dive in.

"Your movements are your jewels. Display each one like a precious gem—take it out of the case, turn it this way and that, catch the light, hand it to the audience and let them admire it. Your dance is a work of art and a gift. You must present it."

We experimented with these dynamics, adding a whole new quality to our work. We imagined we were gift-wrapping our dances like presents for a Christmas morning. Juggling these awarenesses kept me so busy I didn't have time to be nervous. Immersed in the dance and offering it to my imaginary audience, the frightened me with my self-centered fears had no room to exist.

* * *

We'd just arrived for our Friday night rehearsal. "Sit for awhile," Prema motioned us to the pillows on the floor. Leaning my back against the mirror, I wrapped my arms around my knees.

"People love stories, all kinds of stories—adventure stories, love stories, tales of journeys. Our minds want to make meaning. We want to see the shape of our experience. From the time we're born, we're raised on stories. We continue to seek them out as entertainment, education, and spiritual nourishment.

"Our lives are immersed in stories. Even television commercials are thirty-second stories designed to capture our emotions and create the desire for products. We understand our lives through stories. That's why myths come down through the millennia. Stories guide whole cultures and all of the individuals in them. Everyone's living a story. They're the fabric of our history, and of our lives."

Prema shifted her weight as she sat in the chair above us. "How can we use this idea of story to more deeply communicate with our audience?" she asked.

"By acting it out," Rachel volunteered.

"But what if it's an abstract dance that just interprets the musical instruments without a set story line?"

Hearing no response, Prema continued, "Look, we all share the same psychic space. How is it that people get the same idea at the same time in completely different parts of the world? How is it that social movements begin or history changes in a flash? We don't own ideas. They're swirling around us in the air. They're a story whose time has come."

She got up suddenly, "It's interesting to contemplate these things, but we have a performance in three weeks." We started to rise, but she motioned for us to stay. "We've worked on physically communicating with our audience. We've spent a good deal of time learning how to draw them in emotionally. Now how do we communicate on a mental level?"

Eager to hear what she had to say, we remained silent. "By doing your Temple Dance practices, you've all become much more psychic. You each tell me about your extrasensory experiences—mind reading, precognition, and seeing into the past. You've worked on learning to still your mind and project healing thoughts. A couple of you are even able to bring specific qualities and substances into the present moment." Prema seemed pleased by our progress.

"So, can you use your mental abilities to project a story while you dance? I'm not talking about a detailed narrative. I'm talking about a simple mental projection that frames the dance, puts it into a context and sets the scene. Mostly it's a way for you to synchronize yourselves as a group so you have a powerful agreement and a unified focus. Then your dance can be an intentional transmission and not just an entertainment." We listened intently, trying to grasp what Prema was suggesting.

"I'll set the scene for the dances, and then you all transmit the same mental picture and the same emotional tone. Then your performance becomes an inner play, conscious theater. When you add this awareness to your repertoire, it will engage and focus you more."

"It sounds like we're trying to hypnotize the audience," I commented.

"In a way," Prema replied. "Isn't that what we usually do? In conversation, don't we try to make others see our point of view...to agree with how we see a situation?

"I'm designing your performance as an unfolding ritual. Your opening dance creates a sense of pageantry like a festive holiday parade. Mentally you'll be exclaiming, 'Follow me, something big is about to happen.' You want to draw your audience in, take them by visual surprise or by grandeur, seduce them into your world and make them feel that this is a spectacle they shouldn't miss. It's the visual equivalent of saying, 'Once upon a time.'

"You can accomplish this with large props or grand movements or by using music with big orchestration. The key word is pageantry—create a big display, fireworks on a grand scale. The only challenge with this kind of entrance is that then a lot is expected of you. You're committed to following through. To hold the audience you have to continue growing the energy and not slack off.

"Next you'll do the beledi dance, projecting an energetic, earthy quality with your cymbals. You'll each allow yourselves to be seen. You'll become individual personalities whom your audience will want to get to know. Imagine you're a group of friends coming together in your village. Happy to see each other, you share secrets and hopes and dreams and laugh joyously at everything. You do this dance for yourselves as a group. Let the audience watch you play together. The intensity level carries over from your entrance, and the audience is convinced they're in for an adventure.

"So get up now and let's work on these first two dances. Next time I'll set the stories for your other pieces."

Framing the dances in a ritual context made them more powerful—more vital, a living language. We worked for awhile then Prema stopped us. "You need to have time to let this information sink in. Go home and rehearse the dances on your own while projecting these mental images."

I was overwhelmed by the detail that goes into creating an inspiring performance. At home I danced into the wee hours until I truly felt a part of the scenarios that Prema had described.

Turning into Prema's driveway, I stopped short, surprised that I'd arrived so quickly. Caught up in dancing the choreographies in my mind, I hadn't noticed a thing around me. Visions of dances swirled in my head, making it impossible for me to stay in the present moment. I was so afraid I'd forget the steps when we performed.

Letting us in, Prema told us to get our veils and take our places on the floor. She wrapped hers around her shoulders and then looked for a moment at each of us, gathering our attention.

"After your entrance and beledi dance, you want to draw your audience in on a more subtle level. This section of the program literally lifts the veil to the hidden worlds and allows each of you to follow a path to your inner self. And through you, the people in the audience enter their own interior landscapes. If they trust you and are willing to let their guard down, you can lead them on a healing journey.

"As you dance, your isolation movements will open your chakras and clear the energy blocks that are the precursors of disease. And the sheer radiance of the veil will help lift you into the transforming space of Beauty. Ultimately, when you finish this dance, you and your audience will have loosened the crystallized patterns that bind us all to ordinary reality. Everyone will be left with a space for something new to enter.

"Think of the Turkish dervishes. Their whirling is a prayer invoking the Divine. With one hand up to Heaven and the other directed down towards Earth, they allow the energy of the cosmos to move through them. This energy is transformed into whatever's needed in the moment. Their bodies become funnels pouring hope, wonder, and qualities of a more rarified order directly onto the Earth."

I'd seen the Whirling Dervishes of Konya perform the Sema, their ritual dance, during one of their tours through the States. Their continuous turning mesmerized me, but I hadn't really understood their intention. My work with Prema was allowing me to recognize the mystical yearning that inspires them, and I was in awe of their selfless devotion to be of service.

Reminding us that our dancing had the same potential, Prema turned up our veil dance music. With the dervishes as my inspiration and the silk swirling around me, I whirled with rapt attention. During the *taxim*, the slow solo violin section, I held my intention firm, hoping my dancing would be of value.

After several run-throughs, Prema told us to fold our veils. "Next you'll do your drum solo. The drum beckons the spirits and sets up a shared rhythm for all who listen. In other words, by marching to the same drummer, you encourage compassion and empathy. You want to create a community with aspirations and values that are harmonious to one and all. One that allows for the growth of each individual and for the group as a whole."

Prema saw me shaking my head. "What?" she asked.

"I had no idea a performance was packed with so much. I thought people were just dancing."

"Well, mostly they are. That's why many performances are forgotten before the audience even gets home. Rarely do you see conscious performers with very high intentions. Most performers, even those well loved and admired, aren't in touch with these ideas and possibilities. They may have honed their craft but haven't done the inner work needed to make their art a vehicle for something higher."

Quickly searching my mind for performances that had touched me on a soul level, I came up sorely lacking.

"Let's go ahead and talk about the finale," Prema said, "then you can rehearse all the dances in order.

"After you set a unified rhythm through the drum solo, you must give the power back to your audience. You've gathered the energy with your opening dance and have used and controlled it since then. You want to give it back to people in its elevated and transformed state, so they can return to their world and live better, healthier, and more inspired lives.

"For your short finale, you'll travel around as you did in the entrance, but this time you'll return all the attention and energy. Then come forward to take your bows. This allows the audience to express its gratitude and reminds everyone that they've been given a gift, one that should be passed on in some form. And for you as performers, this exchange stimulates you to continue your practices and then come back and share again."

CHAPTER 11:
BRIDE OF THE SPIRIT

While rehearsing for our upcoming performance, each of us designed and sewed pieces of our costumes. We expectantly waited for the arrival of other parts by mail. Anna, a lovely Persian woman who had one of the few bellydance supply shops at that time, was making our skirts from delicate Persian lace fabric shot through with gold and silver metallic threads. We'd each chosen different colors. Mine was a rich royal purple with a red silk underskirt.

To complete my costume, I stitched a gold and multicolored beaded and coined bra to match my belt. I also embroidered a purple vest. My half circular veil was translucent gold with a wide sequin trimmed ruffle. Trying it all on for the first time made me cry. I'd never felt so beautiful.

I rehearsed in front of the mirrors in my otherwise empty living room. Seeing my transformed reflection, I once again understood, on a deep feeling level, the phrase, "The sole purpose of Love is Beauty." Deep into the night I danced my way into ecstasy.

I no longer felt anchored to the Earth. With the stars as my companions, I swirled through the grandeur of the unending Creation. I shimmied in gratitude and joy until the veils dropped from my eyes, and the last vestiges of doubt shook free from my small shuttered reality. I peered into the shimmering Mystery and saw myself—the bride of the Spirit of Dance—unveiled, vulnerable, naked in my finery. Face to face with the Spirit, I was filled with ecstasy. I made my sacred vows and committed myself *till death do us part.*

Meeting for our first dress rehearsal, I could tell the others were also experiencing themselves in a new way. We looked each other over, complimenting our handiwork, sincerely respecting the choices we'd made. We were like sisters in a nunnery, all committed to the same vision.

Prema seemed satisfied with the picture we created as we rehearsed. I found it difficult to keep my mind on all the awarenesses we'd been building. The way the dazzling colors and fabrics transformed the other women distracted me. I felt thrilled to be a part of such beauty.

"You've worked diligently to present your dances on the first three levels of manifestation," Prema said as we stopped to catch our breath. "First," she reviewed, "you've been perfecting your physical technique, learning to use your bodies as vehicles of communication. Secondly, you're imbuing the physical with emotional content. And thirdly, you're projecting a mental picture to frame your dances and create an unfolding story. This combination of focus and perseverance is commendable." Silently we took in her words, realizing what we'd accomplished.

"Through your temple practices, you've prepared your bodies to become vessels for receiving the Spirit. Now, how will you actually make this happen? What haven't we talked about?"

Still contemplating our prior achievements, no one responded.

"Come now," Prema chided, "this is the heart of our whole preparation. What do we need to do? What's missing?"

Filled to the brim, I wondered if I could handle one more task.

"Ask to receive?" Once again Emily bravely came forth with an answer.

"Exactly, get out of the way and ask the Spirit to move through us." Prema beamed at Emily. Then looking intently at each of us, she presented our challenge. "Now you must leave your work behind and take a leap of faith. Trust that all you've learned will be there when you need it. Go unburdened into the moment. Use the dance as a springboard...jump into eternity…unite with the Spirit. Have faith that everything that is necessary, and more, will be provided and will flow right through you into the arms of the audience. You and your performance become the doorway to ecstasy. Let others enter through you."

We prepared to rehearse the show one more time. Before beginning, Prema said, "Throw all thoughts to the wind. Let your mind go and just dance to the music."

Unencumbered by trying to hold on to all the layers of awareness, I felt free. It was heavenly. This is what I'd longed for and dreamed of—the unfettered joy of abandoning myself to the moment.

Later, walking to my car, I wondered if I could be that fearless in front of an audience. I prayed I would have the courage to ask and to trust.

Continuing our rehearsals twice a week, we became tighter as a group, making fewer mistakes and developing a more cohesive unified energy. Prema began creating distractions to see if we could keep our concentration in less controlled situations.

"Turn around, face the back of the room and do the whole show. I want to make sure you're not watching each other in the mirror or cueing off the objects in the room."

"What do you mean?" I asked.

"Well, instead of thinking to turn left, you may have it in your head that you're going toward the stereo. Of course the stereo won't be there on stage. Use verbal cues. Tell yourself what you're actually doing, say right-left-right turn."

Until we tried it ourselves, I thought she was creating a nonexistent problem. My usually keen sense of direction failed me. I was disoriented and kept turning the wrong way. The dances felt totally different. The others were having the same problem, except for Felicia who kept shaking her head at us like we were dummies.

To see if we could maintain our concentration, Prema had us turn and do the show to each side of the room. When we finally pulled ourselves together a bit, she started walking around and talking to us, making jokes and bumping into us as we danced. "There will always be distractions of some sort when you're on stage—a baby cries, a costume tears, one of the other dancers makes a mistake. Will you be able to keep your center?"

On the way back to our cars, we recalled our mishaps and imagined even worse scenarios happening on stage. While I joined the laughter about how klutzy we were, inside I was even more afraid.

D-day was approaching. In my private classes I voiced my fears, but Prema said I shouldn't address them directly, that it would only make them more real. "Sherry, you have to approach your fears from a different angle. You can't solve problems on the same level that they occur on. You have to become a different person, someone who doesn't entertain those negative thoughts.

"Work instead on becoming loveable, transparent, luminous, imbued with a light that attracts others. Become so filled with positive qualities that there's no room for the ones that create fear. All problems are just blockages to the flow of energy. Love is a river. We love an entertainer when she expresses that freedom.

"Remember, the audience will feel as you do. Be boundless. Shatter the barriers you put up to create separation. Become universal. Include everyone in your experience. Performance is not a private endeavor; it's not an egocentric display or a public catharsis. Dance for the world my dear."

CHAPTER 12:
TRIAL BY FIRE

P erformance day finally arrived. It was a sunny, cool, spring afternoon, but I found myself anticipating a baptism by fire. The yearly cultural festival at Santa Barbara's Live Oak Park drew big crowds. The audience sat scrunched together on benches framing three sides of a large stage, while others watched from the shade of a stand of old oak trees.

We stood in a circle backstage with pinky fingers entwined. In a low but majestic voice Prema began her invocation, "We ask that we be allowed to dance for the world. We trust that whatever is needed in this moment will flow through us. We are grateful to be vessels for the Most High." We squeezed our fingers together, affirming her words. Then as Prema had instructed earlier, we stood silently waiting to be announced.

As a large company of Greek dancers took their final bows, I worked vigilantly on my state of mind. I was shaking enough to set my coins jingling, but I was careful about what I allowed into my mind. Every time a fearful word tried to surface, I took a deep breath and countered with, "Performing is a piece of cake," or, "I love people watching me dance."

I was so busy talking to myself that I didn't hear us being introduced. But as our music began, I followed Felicia, Rachel, and Emily out. I felt like I was being shot out of a cannon and catapulted onto center stage. Adrenaline roared through my body. The sun blinded me, but the welcoming applause of the crowd left no doubt that they were out there with all eyes on us.

Feeling stunned, I didn't have a clue what the next step was, but luckily muscle memory clicked in. Stealing a quick glance, I seemed to be doing the same steps as the others. I took a deep breath and let the air out in little sputters. Time shifted...

I must have been moving in and out of the present moment, because we were already into our second dance. I was amazed to hear my finger cymbals tapping away as my body changed lines with the other dancers.

Felicia smiled at me and winked. I remember thinking, "Will wonders never cease." We changed patterns again, and I saw Rachel using her eyes and expressions with a presence that compelled the audience to watch.

Prema had impressed upon us that we were all at different levels in our performing experience, so she didn't expect the same things from each of us. Felicia and Rachel, as more seasoned performers, had the responsibility of engaging the audience and being the central focus. Emily's job was to work on her stage presence, remembering to project feelings with her face and movements.

As a first time performer, my mission was to try to be present on stage if only for just a few moments. "Even one deep breath is a great start," Prema said. "Inexperienced performers are usually overwhelmed by having so much energy focused on them. They have out-of-body experiences and come offstage muttering, 'What just happened?'

"Your job is to try to have a conscious moment—one that you remember. You want to start building a history of stage time and realize that not only did you survive, but you may even have enjoyed yourself. You don't want to start from zero each time feeling like it's your first performance." Prema winked at me, "You can only be a virgin once!"

And now, while spinning inside my golden veil, I had my second conscious moment. I remembered learning this movement for the first time and the feeling of accomplishment I had when I finally did it correctly. I took a deep breath and told myself, "Now here I am onstage performing." I didn't surface again, though, until we were taking our bows. I heard the audience applauding and realized that the performance was over.

Prema met us as we came offstage and urged us to stop and listen. The audience was still cheering. Soaking in the sound of their applause, we all spoke at once. We laughed about how the wind blew our veils around our faces and the sun reflected off our crystal beads, blinding us. We chattered on about running into each other while changing lines, about forgetting steps, and about turning the wrong way. But we could tell from their reaction that the audience hadn't even been aware of these minor mishaps.

Prema let us run on for a few moments then put the brakes on, "Take the energy and instead of blowing it all away, give yourselves a moment to go over the performance in your mind. Realize what you did well and what you need to work on for next time. Set your intention for the next performance and infuse it with the charged elevated energy from this show. This is a special energy—it's a subtle substance that will help you manifest your vision."

I walked away from the others and rested against a tree. Its limbs shaded me from the bright afternoon sun. I mentally reviewed the few conscious moments I'd had onstage. They were fleeting but memorable; they had a rarified quality. At that point I could only wish for more.

As a result of our success, we were invited to appear at many other events. We danced outside on the streets at arts and crafts festivals, on stage at elegant charity benefits, and at opening parties for the opera season. We also entertained at university functions and volunteered on a regular basis to perform at nursing facilities and homes for the elderly.

Like learning to dance, learning to perform didn't unfold in a linear way. Each performance was a completely unique experience. There were so many variables—the venue itself, the other acts, our place in the lineup, the time of day, the audience size and type of people.

Each performance was a new initiation. I'd set my intention and go out and see what I could accomplish. Could I breathe more? Could I let my emotions be visible on my face? Could I maintain my posture? Could I remember the small details, like beautiful hands and feet? Like life, each performance was an opportunity to see if I could meet the moment in an open way.

I did all this from the relative safety of my little neophyte cocoon. While the other dancers took care of the audience, I had the luxury of just being concerned with myself. Soon though, it was time for me to acknowledge the audience and take some responsibility for the entertainment value of our performance.

I began to set my intention to consciously engage the audience. Could I look out and see one person? Could I take in the whole crowd? Could I see them and be aware of them seeing me? Just when I thought I'd finally overcome my stage fright and that I was perfecting the choreography, I'd find myself backstage once more shaking in my dance sandals.

I began to realize that like life, dance and performance are never ending learning processes. Sometimes in my fear and lack of trust, I'd get stuck in old limited ideas and shut down. But when I left the door open and did the work, a transcendent feeling of ecstasy graced me.

These moments reminded me of Brigadoon, the magical land that's only approachable by ordinary folks once every hundred years. I feared that if I didn't take the opportunity that was offered, the door might close and not open again for me in this lifetime. I intensified my practices as an invitation to more frequent visitations. I didn't want to miss my one and only chance.

I was completely consumed by the dance. At home I listened to Middle Eastern music from morning till night. It spoke to me, urging me to translate sound into movement. I'd be making a piece of jewelry, but unable to sit still, I'd rise and dance for hours.

The dance muse was even more demanding than my jewelry muse. It would awaken me in the middle of the night, strains of music filling my body, lifting me from my bed and drawing me out to the living room.

There I'd stand completely still until I was compelled to move. Feeling a subtle pulsing, I'd begin to sway...the movement slowly developing into graceful fluid gestures. They'd continue growing until my balance shifted, transforming them into something entirely different.

Finally I'd be pushed from my spot on the floor and find myself traveling around the empty, mirrored room. I'd watch my reflection float by, an apparition lit by the moonlight shining through the window. It was a love affair—the music, the dance and I becoming one.

It was as if I understood a foreign language and could speak like a native. I intuited the structures of the classical and modern Egyptian compositions and could easily translate their complex patterns into dance. The instruments told me how they wished to appear.

I realized that I now had a new medium to create with, and the jewelry was no longer my chosen language of expression. I'd made a good living and had clients around the country who waited for my new designs each year. I would be disappointing them when I didn't return to show my work. But I'd committed myself to living a life with heart, and my heart was now completely possessed by the dance.

I knew there was no going back.

I'd arrived at my last class in a disheveled state. I was still struggling with the physical pressure of the excessive energy that continued to overwhelm me; it seemed to be building rather than abating. I was only at ease while I was dancing. The rest of the time I felt beside myself. I wished I could jump out of my skin.

Seeing the state I was in, Prema had suggested I visit a woman in town who might help me explore the deeper reasons for my predicament. She warned me that Gabie used some unusual means to get at a person's true self, and that I should keep an open mind.

Scheduled to meet Gabie, I drove through the Arbolata, Ojai's upscale neighborhood with its sprawling homes nestled on manicured green lawns. Just paying the water bill to keep the landscaping lush in this heat meant the owners had to be of substantial means. I continued up the hill toward the mountaintop and turned into a steep driveway.

I don't know what I was expecting, but I was surprised to be met by such a normal looking woman. She ushered me into her sedate serene home and introduced me to her husband. He sat in front of a window calmly watching several plump-bellied sparrows flip their tiny wings around in the bowl of an ornately carved birdbath. A jagged bundle of nerves, I couldn't imagine how he managed to be so relaxed.

I wanted to stay and watch, but Gabie led me down a hallway and into a small study. Inviting me to sit on a big overstuffed armchair, she sat opposite me and asked if I had something personal that she could hold in her hand. "One of the methods I use is psychometry," she explained. "When I hold an object that belongs to a person, I can see their past, present, and often their future."

"It's not fortunetelling," she replied to my raised eyebrows, "it's an investigation. Examining parts of ourselves that we don't consciously remember can help us to know who we truly are. Once you know yourself, your path becomes clear and you can do the work only you were born to do."

I took the gold bracelet that I'd made and wore everyday, from my wrist and handed it to her. She folded her fingers over it as she closed her eyes and exhaled slowly...

"You're in a time of crisis," she began. "You've been in this same position many times in past lives and always turned away from the path that would set you free." Speaking naturally, she continued, "Once again you're at a crossroads. One way will allow you an easy life of conventional activities that maintain the status quo. The other will require sacrifice, study, and service."

She stopped for a moment, rubbing her empty hand up and down her chest. She seemed distressed and I feared she was having a heart attack, but then she spoke again. "You're experiencing a pressure that is trying to push you in a more evolved direction. It's not the energy that makes you uncomfortable and scared; it's your resistance. You're creating a dam and the pressure is building. If you can just let go and accept this new course, you'll find an equilibrium. Or," she paused briefly, "just say *no* and the door will be closed again until another lifetime."

I felt the truth in what she said, but it seemed so general that it could have applied to anyone. She was waiting for me to respond.

I shrugged, "But I have no idea what my path is."

Handing my bracelet back, she asked if I was willing to try something that might reveal a clue to my life's work. "This method I use is called past life regression. We can go back and explore your previous lives and see if we find a pattern that connects them." I was afraid that she wanted to hypnotize me and that I'd be giving my mind over to her. She assured me that I would be completely conscious and could stop whenever I liked.

"Relax and close your eyes…breathe naturally." After a time, she asked, "Where are you?"

I was just about to say, "right here," when I saw myself as a young girl streaking across a once-familiar landscape…

I'm running across a grassy lawn through a water sprinkler. I hop onto the porch of the house in Virginia where I live. I dash through the living room, up the steep stairway, into my parents' room. I jump onto their bed and into my mother's pillow, which opens like a door to receive me.

I hurry down massive carved stone steps, which become larger and larger as I shrink smaller and smaller. Down, down, down I go trying to keep from falling into the cracks between the stones. I reach the bottom landing and look around to get my bearings.

Everything is so huge. I can't tell where I am. I see a light and move toward it. I slip through a slit beneath a door into a vast cavern of a room. Two men are bending over a table in the center of the chamber. A shaft of light illuminates the table but leaves the rest in shadow.

As my eyes focus, I see figures wrapped in white fabric propped up in wooden boxes that line the walls of the room. Startled, I realize that they're mummies and that the men at the table are preparing another mummy, slowly winding the gauze-like fabric around the unclothed body of a man.

As I move back in horror, one of the men notices me and rushes towards me. I frantically dart around the room screaming, "I don't want to be a mummy. I don't want to be a mummy." I scurry as fast as my little legs will carry me up the gigantic steps, out the pillow, down the stairs, through the banging screen door and onto the lawn. My heart is pounding, but I'm grateful to be alive. In a totally conscious moment, I realize that I have to stay aware or face being turned into a mummy in this life. At the young age of five, I know that all is not as it seems.

I could hear Gabie telling me to open my eyes and asking if I remembered what I'd just experienced. Not only did I remember, but this was a very familiar and terrifying recurring dream I had as a child. Whenever I told people about my dream, they wondered how a five year old would even know so much about Egypt and mummies. Night after night I would have this dream, and though the adults told me it wasn't real, I knew it was.

"Would you like to explore further?" Gabie inquired. "It's obvious that your memory had great significance to intrude so forcefully into the life of a small child." I took a deep breath and another vision came into focus…

I'm a young woman dancing in a temple sanctuary surrounded by tall columns and walls painted with hieroglyphics. My parents have dedicated me to the temple to become a priestess and serve the gods.

"Move further along in that life," I heard Gabie say.

I see vast crowds of people gathered around a tomb. The pharaoh has just died and I'm to be buried alive, one of the handmaidens to serve him on his journey. I'm completely panic-stricken.

Gabie again told me to move ahead. To my surprise, I found myself alive and living out a life of great luxury. I backtracked a bit and saw that my beauty and influence with the guards, one of whom helped me escape, had saved me.

"Move ahead into the next lifetime," Gabie suggested. Here I also found myself dancing, this time in ancient India. Once more I was dedicated to a temple and performed the Bharata Natyam, the sacred temple dance. And once again I garnered favor with a man, the son of a rajah, who had come to ask blessings for his royal family. Taking me away from the temple, he made me his favored concubine.

Moving ahead again, I found myself in similar situations in Persia and then in Constantinople. Each time I came to a crossroads where I could have chosen to use my beauty, charisma, and talents as a dancer to heal and uplift the spirits of the people. But each time my wild and selfish nature ruled. When given the opportunity, rather than fulfill my duties, I left the temples. I chose to enjoy lives of privilege and self-indulgence rather than sacrifice my personal desires.

Gabie called me fully back into the present, and I opened my eyes. Taking in my surroundings, I was surprised to find myself in the same small room I had entered a couple of hours ago.

"Did you get what you came here for?" Gabie asked.

"I'm beginning to get the picture," I replied. I remembered everything I'd seen. Part of me wanted to call the whole thing a giant fantasy, but a feeling in my gut told me these were actual memories.

As I left, Gabie gave me an audiotape of the session. She suggested that instead of wondering if these visions were really past lives, I should explore how they shed light on my present life.

I stopped on the way down the mountain and looked out over the valley. Here I was once again learning the Temple Dance, and though not in a formal temple, I was being asked to use the dance and my life to serve others.

The next day I drove out to Creek Road and sat by the trickling stream. Two horseback riders from the country club threaded their way through the trees, nodding to me as they passed by. I wondered how they could seem so peaceful in the wake of the storm I felt raging all around and inside of me. Life was in total chaos—was I the only one who could see that everything was falling apart? I watched the horses splash through the water and climb up the trail on the other side, disappearing around the bend.

Contemplating my meeting with Gabie, I tried to see this lifetime and my past lives as a blueprint of my destiny. As a child I'd been extremely empathetic, deeply experiencing the emotions of all those around me. I wanted to save the world. But because of family circumstances, I'd changed. I learned how to shut down so I wouldn't feel other peoples' pain and sorrow. My goal became getting away from my family and leading a glamorous life where I didn't have to think about anyone but myself. I became a self-involved person. Now I was again being asked to put others' needs before my own.

I wished all of these insights would disappear so I could get back to my old life with only myself to think about. If I accepted my recent experiences as real, I'd have to change my whole conception of life. As much as I was suffering, I still wanted to hold on to my old ideas and desires. I searched desperately for a rational explanation, but the more I held on, the more confused I got. My mind was reeling. Feeling totally out of control, I jumped up and ran to my car.

I can't remember how I got there, but I found myself in the lush garden of the Ranch House, a well-known gourmet restaurant favored by Hollywood celebrities. The owners, Alan and Helen, were rubbing my hands and trying to get me to drink chamomile tea. They said I'd raced in all freaked out and crying in a state of distress and confusion. I tried to tell them what was happening to me, but I must have sounded incoherent. They said it was Good Friday and urged me to come home with them until I calmed down.

Taking me to their home, they put me to bed. I slept through the night and was embarrassed to find myself still there in the morning. I quickly got myself together to leave. As I passed through the kitchen where they were having breakfast, Helen stopped me and asked where I was going. With tears rolling down my face, I said I had no idea where to go or what to do. Alan insisted I join them.

Reluctantly I sat. Alan stopped buttering his toast and said, "A very wise man once told me that 'choice is confusion.' Any move that you make from a state of confusion will have adverse consequences. Please stay here until you're clear that there's no choice about your next step."

"How will I know?"

"You'll know what to do when you know who you are.

"But I don't even know where to begin."

"You might contemplate who you are without all the ideas you have about yourself and life."

All that day I sat alone in their garden. The energy running through my body was stronger and more distressing than ever, and my mind was running rampant. I watched the koi swimming lazily around the stone rimmed pond, but nothing calmed me.

I tried to observe myself. Like Ishtar, I desperately clung to the veils that kept me wrapped in the dark burial chamber of my rational mind. I was terrified to let go of my illusions and stand naked in the face of Life and Death. Who would I be? What would my life be like? I'd struggled with this torment for so long, and I was still fiercely holding on, hoping for some logical resolution to my dilemma. I was afraid I would lose my mind and go stark raving mad. But I'd finally reached the end of my rope.

As the sun went down, I dragged myself back to the guest room and crawled into bed. Lying there with the covers pulled over my head, I finally pleaded, "God, if you're there, please help me." I didn't know who I was anymore and I felt like I was dying. Huddled in a fetal position, I shook so hard I finally exhausted myself. I fell asleep afraid that I wouldn't wake up in the morning.

During the night I dreamt of the Resurrection, though it was I who rose from the dead. Surrounded by blinding light, I walked naked from my tomb. Cleansed and purified of my past, I welcomed the dawn of a new day. I was unbound, free, reborn.

When I awoke it was Easter morning. The sun was out, the birds were singing, the daffodils and tulips were blossoming, and I was at peace. Just like that.

I didn't understand what had happened. How, after all this time, did the fear and anguish vanish overnight? Looking out the window, I saw Alan pruning roses in the garden. I walked through the French doors into a little piece of paradise. Yesterday I'd been so wrapped up in myself, I hadn't seen the order and perfection that was right in front of me. Today, I could only marvel at the beauty of God's creation.

Alan beamed at me.

I just shook my head in wonder.

"There's a time for every flower to bloom," he said softly.

He gently cupped a fragile bud in his large hand. "Just imagine the energy and pressure in this rose before the petals open. Think of the scent and the beauty held tightly within, yearning to show itself to the world. Does the rose resist it's transformation from bud to flower? If so, it too must suffer."

He snipped off a perfect red rose and held it toward me. I reached out and took its exquisite beauty in my palm. Raising it to my nose, I inhaled the fragrant fulfillment of its promise.

Alan smiled at me like a loving father. "You were like this rose...waiting to blossom."

Drinking in the velvety petals and intoxicating scent, I knew once again that the sole purpose of Love is Beauty.

INITIATION IV:

THE WAY OF TEACHING

CHAPTER 13:
OUT OF THE NEST

D riving out to the East End, I experienced Ojai as I had the very first time I saw it. Without the dark curtain of fear clouding my vision, it looked like the first day of Creation. The valley was surely Eden and I the innocent Eve.

Delighted to see me at peace with myself, Prema wasted no time. The next step in my evolution, she said, was to teach others what I'd learned. "It's time to see if you can keep your intention and stay centered amidst the ten thousand things. With your new set of eyes, go see what's happening out there in the big world. Make yourself available and see where you're led. Surely there are people out there waiting and hoping for you to teach them a thing or two."

"But where will I go?" I asked reluctantly.

"When you put yourself in the path of service, the way will always open up for you," Prema replied.

I would have been happy to stay indefinitely in Ojai, continuing my training and performing with the Shakti Dancers. But Prema was pushing me out of the nest; she said I needed to test my wings. Everything seemed to conspire to send me on my way. I felt centered and strong. I couldn't make excuses.

Finally I agreed to hit the road and follow my intuition. I put a few things in Little Chief Rolling Hills, my trusty yellow Volkswagen bug. Putting my tapes and boom box in the back seat, I laughed. Making and selling my jewelry required all kinds of tools, equipment, and a big display. For dancing I simply needed an empty room, a mirror, and a sound system. Placing Lily Trueheart in her pet taxi on the passenger seat, off I went. My intention was to keep traveling until I found the right place to teach.

Some of the people I knew told me I was crazy to give up a lucrative business that gave me so much freedom. Fearing I'd never make it teaching such an unusual practice, they urged me to reconsider and stay with my safe and familiar life. But I was committed to my new path, and I felt I had to heed Prema's guidance.

I drove up the California coast through Oregon and then into Washington where I took a ferry to my first destination, the tiny coastal town of Port Townsend. Old friends I'd been out of touch with had called on the same day Prema told me it was time to go. They'd moved to Port Townsend and invited me to visit. Taking that as a clear sign, I set my intention. If I liked the area and it was receptive to me—meaning everything flowed smoothly—I would stay. Otherwise I'd move on.

I liked the town immediately. It was small and felt protected like Ojai. I loved wandering around. Ornate, gingerbread Victorian houses sat uptown on a bluff overlooking the waterfront. Below, shops and restaurants lined the downtown street along Puget Sound. And after living like a hermit for so long and going through such a difficult time, it was nice being with friends.

After a week of getting a feel for the town, I stopped by a local property manager's office and told her I wanted to check out a house I'd noticed with a For Rent sign in its window. Trying to discourage me, she said it was old, in disrepair, and had no furniture. She wanted to show me a cute little furnished apartment. "You should at least have a warm cozy home," she urged. But I insisted.

We pulled up in front of the old Victorian with its curling blue paint. Unlocking the front door, she led me from the foyer to the living room and then into the dining room where I stopped short in disbelief. In the otherwise completely empty room, one wall was lined with mirrors, and a stereo with two large speakers sat on a low corner table.

Seeing my shocked expression, the realtor was taken aback. "What did you see?" she whispered. "They say this place is haunted. Did you see a ghost?" Shaking my head, I followed her quickly around the rest of the house. She was anxious to leave but allowed me to stay so I could get a feeling for the place.

The moment she left I started laughing nervously, then slid down the wall and sat giggling on the floor. It was clear that life was just one big mirror, and I was being handed exactly what I needed. I imagined moving in immediately and beginning small classes. I got up and twirled across the floor.

The idea that our thoughts are creative became an obvious living reality. That they could be as specific as finding mirrors and a stereo, in the first house I looked at, still surprised me. I could only take it as a sign that this was where I was meant to be. I was sure I'd found my new home and studio.

While waiting to hear if the landlord would make the necessary repairs, I began teaching private classes in a local dance studio. Like many small towns, anything new was either quickly embraced or looked at suspiciously. Fortunately, people were intrigued with the notion of bellydance as a spiritual practice. Unfortunately, I immediately came face to face with the reality of being the teacher rather than the student.

It wasn't the students who were the problem; it was my own expectations of myself. My students had an uncanny knack for asking the only things I thought I didn't know. As I struggled for answers, I became alarmingly aware of just how much that was.

After my night classes, I'd fall into a disturbed sleep, certain that I was a fake. Overcome with self-doubt, I began having my lost tape dreams...

In the studio before class, I'm preparing for my students. I look for my tapes to put them in the order of play, but I can't find them. I search again and still no tapes. Meanwhile, the students are filtering in. They stand around, politely waiting. I frantically dig through my things and still no tape. More people come in. I'm thinking that this is my one and only chance to attract these students, and I'm blowing it—I don't have music to play. The room fills with people. They're getting restless. Some start to leave. Finally, I find an old tape at the bottom of my bag, and though it isn't appropriate warm-up music, I put it on and take my place in front of the class. The music is totally wrong, but it doesn't matter now anyway. Almost everyone has left, so they don't even hear the tape snap. I stand alone listening to the derogatory comments of the last few students as they quickly walk away.

After a couple of weeks of this recurring nightmare, I finally called Prema. Ashamed to admit that her faith in me had been sorely misplaced, I babbled on about my inadequacies as a teacher. When I paused for a moment she calmly stated, "It's all in the dance."

Asking her repeatedly to explain the questions that had stumped me, she only replied, "Sherry, it's all in the dance."

Frustrated, I told her I would never know enough to teach, and she said, "It's all in the dance."

More and more irritated with her refusal to answer me, I finally just whimpered, "What should I say when I don't know the answers?"

Again she replied, "It's all in the dance." Then pausing, she added, "Don't say a thing."

"Oh." *Of course,* I thought, *why say anything?* Hearing Prema's words, my worries instantly fell away. I'd been trying to tell people things that could only be known through experience, yet all of the experience was in the dance, not in the words. From my own search, I knew this intimately. Grateful once again for Prema's wisdom, I wondered aloud how I might remember her words. I was afraid this revelation might slip away.

"Sherry," Prema answered, "remember that gratitude is the key to Will. Before they begin turning, the Whirling Dervishes ask Allah if they might be allowed to turn. Before your classes, always ask, 'May I be allowed to teach?' In this way you'll never be alone. You'll know that I'm there with you, and that you also have the support and guidance of all those who have ever practiced in this way. As part of a living tradition, the power and wisdom of those who have come before will forever be available to you. And always remember to say *thank you.*"

I stayed in Port Townsend for another month, teaching my classes and trying to rent the old Victorian. But the owner refused to do repairs. Finding it had seemed like providence, but it was still out of reach. Once again I dialed Prema. It was great to hear her voice. I told her about my problems renting the house and asked her advice.

"Time, place, and circumstance have to be right for the correct thing to happen," she answered. "The time may be right, and the circumstance, but apparently the place is not."

"But what about the mirrors and the stereo," I asked, "aren't they a sign?"

"They may have been a sign, but not necessarily that you're supposed to live there."

"I don't get it," I said. "How will I ever know what things actually mean?"

"Just ask yourself three questions."

"You're kidding, right?" I laughed, thinking she sounded like a genie in a bottle.

"You must ask three questions," she repeated. I could feel her sternness penetrating through the phone line.

"Please tell me," I implored, realizing she was serious.

"In every circumstance, when you want to know what to do, or need to decide whether to offer someone advice, or try to heal them, or in any way influence their life…"

I waited anxiously.

"Ask: Can I? Should I? May I?"

Recalling the childhood game of *Mother May I* that we played as kids, I asked, "What if I'm not sure of the answer to any of those questions?"

"That's exactly the point," she responded. "Remember, I once told you that *yes is yes…no is no…and maybe is no?* If you're unsure, something about the situation isn't conducive to a satisfactory resolution. *Maybe means no!*"

Prema's simple words were profoundly liberating. "Sherry, if you don't have a positive feeling about something now, while it's right in front of you, you won't have the energy to sustain it over time or to see it through. If you ask these questions when trying to help someone and get a *no* or a *maybe*, you may be feeling that person's resistance to change, or perhaps even to you."

Letting go of the idea that the mirrors and stereo were an undeniable sign to open a studio in Port Townsend, I asked Prema's three questions. I immediately realized that the town was too small and too remote for building a teaching practice that could support me. And besides, being the California sun worshiper that I'd become, I was freezing in the constantly overcast weather. Packing up Little Chief Rolling Hills, I put Lily Trueheart in her pet taxi and headed south for warmer climes.

CHAPTER 14:
IN SEARCH OF MY TRIBE

W inding my way back down through Oregon, I checked out places that people mentioned might be receptive to my vision. I passed through college towns like Eugene and artsy towns like Ashland with its yearly Shakespearean festival. They were strong contenders but not right for various reasons.

I continued into California to Mount Shasta then swung east to Lake Tahoe. I considered the possibilities, but again, the town didn't seem right. I decided to visit one of my sisters in Nevada City. She'd just moved into the carriage house of an estate where the main residence was used for meetings and classes.

Strolling around the grounds the next morning, I was surprised to hear strains of Egyptian folkloric music drifting out the screen door of a basement room. Seven women were taking a bellydance class. As I opened the door, the teacher beckoned me to join them. Slipping inside, I instantly became part of a sisterhood that practices the same movements the world over. Nothing was said until the end of class when I was greeted like a long lost family member. The feeling of belonging to a tightknit though scattered tribe reconfirmed my intentions.

I continued down through the southwest and then headed east. Looking for signs of bellydancers everywhere I stopped, I found and attended classes across the country. Like a secret society, they were hard to find. I felt like an archeologist looking for traces of an almost extinct species. I had a few leads but mostly had to be a good detective. I'd roll into a town and start by calling dance studios listed in the Yellow Pages. I'd contact community centers, following clues until I found someone who knew someone, who knew someone else, who studied bellydance.

At that time you couldn't find bellydance and other ethnic dance classes in mainstream studios. They were always held in some out of the way pocket, like an oasis in the desert. I'd leave the motel where I was staying and set out across town or into the countryside searching for my tribe. Sure that I was hopelessly lost, I would eventually find the address I was seeking and hear strains of Middle Eastern music. I'd run in late and quickly join a class already in session.

In those moments, I was home, I could relax. The music, the jingling coins and sparkling sequins, the familiar movements and unusual array of costumes assured me I was on the right path. Welcoming, inquisitive faces wondered who I was, where I'd come from, and what tales I had to tell about the bellydance family in other regions.

Each class was unique. In Santa Fe, New Mexico I spent the evening with a very polished troupe that was rehearsing for an upcoming performance. In Steamboat Springs, Colorado I took a beginner class in an old farmhouse. In Brown County, Indiana, I learned new veil moves.

I was zigzagging my way east to a retreat center in upstate New York. Omega Institute offered workshops in the arts and spiritual studies, along with cutting edge human potential and self-help seminars. Participants from all over the world came during the summer months to explore subjects they couldn't find in mainstream institutions. I was delighted to find that my unusual interests fit right in.

In exchange for working, I was invited to stay at their rustic lakefront retreat for the summer. My job was answering phones at their reception desk.

Asked to give bellydance lessons for the staff, I taught a group of women and a few men in one of the open-air studios. The class was a great success, and this time I felt confident while teaching and loved sharing my knowledge. As the summer progressed, we began preparing to perform for the closing weekend celebration.

And so my first troupe, the Omega Dancers, was born. They were receptive and dedicated, quickly absorbing the challenging technique. I taught them a veil dance and a drum solo, which we rehearsed nightly after finishing our day jobs.

This was at a time long before you could find a hundred sites on the internet selling bellydance supplies. We dyed our own veils cut from white silk. Then we drove the forty-five minutes to a Woodstock thrift store to buy bits and pieces for creating our costumes. We ended up looking like an exotic, if somewhat ragtag band of gypsies. We entertained hundreds of people to great reviews. Not bad for my first troupe. I loved it.

As an added benefit of being the leader, I didn't have the luxury of indulging in stage fright. My job was to be the one encouraging my students to relax and enjoy. After struggling for so long with anxiety and lack of confidence, I really relished the role of fearless leader. I had no lost tape nightmares, but I did have a few lost costume dreams.

Leaving Omega in the fall, I picked up Lily Trueheart. She had become the reigning queen of Blueberry Hill, my friends' farm in Massachusetts. Sleeping with Heather and Lewis, my little furry pal had displaced their two dogs and three cats, commandeering the pillows at the head of the bed. She reluctantly allowed me to tuck her into her pet taxi, then we set out toward the South to visit people I'd met at Omega. They had enthusiastically arranged for me to teach dance workshops for their friends at home.

Introducing the dance, and making it fun and accessible on a one-shot basis, gave me a lot of new challenges. I learned to read a group on the spot and present what I felt was needed in each place. I could see why certain people formed friendships and what would take their relationships to another level. Some people just needed something more interesting to do together. Some needed new ideas to open up their worlds. Still others needed to respect each other and shift from being catty to being supportive. I didn't have a standard class I gave over and over. Sometimes it was slow temple movement, sometimes it was shake it loose and get it in gear.

I always remembered Prema's guidance—that it's all in the dance. The dance became the point to rally the group around. Most of the people had never even seen live bellydance and were surprised and delighted at how quickly and deeply it affected them.

The workshop experiences reinforced my commitment to allow no judgment or competition in my classes. I taught the dance as a way for all of us to come into deeper relationship with our selves, our fellow dancers, and our lives. I experimented with different ways to engage the attention of people of assorted ages, types, and learning styles. I found that though each class was unique, the elements were similar. The classes were a ritual arranged around a structure that allowed each student to experience her own life energy and let her spirit soar. It was exciting and gratifying to find that I had become a catalyst for change. The circles at the end of each workshop revealed a group of beaming, open, and connected people.

I returned to Ojai nine months later—a gestation period but still no baby. I had no studio and no idea where I would settle though I'd traveled full circle, some eight thousand miles around the country.

Thrilled to be back in the valley and to see Prema, I was bursting to tell my tales of the road. She greeted me warmly and listened intently, nodding, making astute comments, and helping me to understand what I'd actually learned. I knew once again how grateful I was to have found such a wise teacher and realized that I had come to love her deeply.

Prema had been asked to teach a class in Ventura, a town twelve miles from Ojai on the coast. She suggested I teach the class; it would give me good experience and I'd be able to continue my studies with her.

On the first night of class, I was pleased to find a group of fourteen women. Instructing an ongoing class promised to be a completely different lesson for me than the short classes and workshops I'd been teaching. I would have to consider the continuing development of each dancer, and of the group as a whole, if I hoped to inspire them to make a deep commitment to dance as a spiritual practice.

Seeing them on a regular basis, I began to learn about my students and their personal histories. Each one of them taught me valuable life lessons. A woman named Carla taught me what I most needed to learn. She lived with her husband and his ailing mother. While he went to work every day, Carla took care of her mother-in-law. To make ends meet, she was registered at six different talent agencies that sent her out to do bellygrams.

Every day she would get up, put on full makeup, and lay out her costumes. She had three different acts. One was a traditional bellydance show and one was a magic act. Her third show combined the two—dressed like *I Dream of Genie*, she danced and did magic tricks.

Carla would be at home when a call came to do an impromptu performance. Asking the neighbor to keep an ear out for her mother-in-law, she'd dress and speed off to entertain and to create beauty. She danced an average of six or seven times a week, sometimes a couple of shows a day.

She gave me a photograph of herself in costume. She looked so polished and professional, I could barely tell it was the same woman who came to class. I felt embarrassed when she wrote on the photo how much joy my teaching brought to her life. I was just teaching her beginning bellydance, while she was teaching me how to grow lotuses out of mud. She was a glowing example of how to live with determination and without self-pity. She inspired me to want to create beauty no matter what circumstances I found myself in, and she showed me how to be grateful no matter how difficult life seemed.

$*\ *\ *$

Soon after the series of classes ended, I was invited to share space in a dance studio opening in the San Francisco Bay area. The studio was near downtown Sausalito, a charming little town just over the Golden Gate Bridge. Traveling north to check it out, I found the studio light and airy and the owner's vision in harmony with mine. I was overjoyed to feel that my long search was over.

I scheduled two classes a day, morning and night, although I didn't have a clientele. To keep my practice going and also create the energy and atmosphere to attract new students, I committed to holding my classes even if no one came. Kind of like 'if you build it they will come.' While waiting for students to show up, I gave myself many a class.

Finally one morning a head peeked in the open doorway. Attracted by the music, a young woman with finely sculpted features and long black hair asked what I was doing. I invited her in to take a free introductory class. She said she'd just put her clothes in the laundromat around the corner and could stay for the half hour until she had to move them into the dryer.

Cheryl was very receptive and responsive as I began to teach her the basics. She left to put her wash in the dryer and then returned to finish her class. Between the wash and dry cycle, I finally found a student. She was my first and longest staying pupil, beginning a steady stream that hasn't abated for over thirty years.

Soon after, I formed my first ongoing troupe, The Mystic East Dancers. Then I decided that it was time for me to head to the source of the dance. I needed to go to Egypt.

INITIATION V:

RETURN TO THE SOURCE

CHAPTER 15:
WELCOME HOME

I awoke to the sound of a baby crying. It was still dark as I opened the window shade of the packed 747. The map projected on the movie screen showed we were somewhere over the Mediterranean speeding toward the coast of North Africa. My first waking thought was that we didn't have flying machines the last time I was in Egypt. Then I realized that I'd never actually been there before, only in my dreams and visions. It was the ancient land that I remembered.

As the sky grew lighter, I gazed at the sea below, trying to read the past in its steely surface. I pondered time and space and the nature of so-called reality. Had I actually lived here centuries before? Was reincarnation real?

Suddenly I saw land. Like a mother seeing her child's profile for the first time, the outline of the Dark Continent struck me with wonder. As the sun came up, I could see a waterway curling through the emptiness of the desert sands. Tears flowed like the river down my cheeks. I thought then that the Nile must be filled with the tears of joy of all those people who felt they were finally coming home.

We circled for our landing. Amidst the confusion of a city sprawling out to the edges of the desert, I saw a sight so fantastic and yet so familiar. Like sand dunes with an attitude, the triangular faces of the three pyramids at Giza stood shadowed in the long morning light. When I saw the Sphinx sitting guard like Krishna at Prema's door, I became aware of just how far I'd traveled.

A stream of pictures having nothing to do with my present life flooded my consciousness, fading only with the jolt of our wheels on the runway. Though I knew we had landed in Cairo, I felt like an alien arriving on an unexplored planet. Then we were out the door of the plane into an airport setting that rivaled the Space Bar scene in Star Wars. All kinds of characters sat, walked, lounged and lay in an undulating mob. The loud din in a variety of languages and dialects evoked the tower of Babel.

Veiled women, blanket wrapped Bedouins, Saudi Arabian mustached men in checkered headdresses, chic women in designer clothes and stiletto heels, hippies in tie-dyed shirts, serious looking travelers with hiking boots and backpacks. Hundreds of people all milled around at six in the morning.

Competing for the good will of rushing travelers, beggars sprawled on the shiny marble floor. A mother with three ragged children clustered around her was nursing the fourth child in her arms. Blind men with cups. Monks with bowls. Amputees in rags. Humanity in all its guises. It was overwhelming.

As we huddled together, I checked out my traveling companions. Our dance tour of Egypt had been arranged by Morocco—a renowned bellydance instructor from New York. We were eleven women dancers and one husband, coming from all over the United States. Tired from the California to New York leg of my journey, I'd spoken just briefly to one of the women, Khalidah, who sat next to me on the transatlantic flight. After exchanging names she put a blanket over her head and promptly fell asleep, awakening only when we landed.

A young Egyptian guide, dressed in a western business suit, greeted Morocco in fluent English. Introducing himself as Hassan, he herded our group to baggage claim and then on to customs. Once through the line, we boarded a minibus and began the journey to our hotel.

Leaving the airport, we were immediately thrust into a free-for-all. It seemed at first that there was no organization; the traffic was careening this way and that. Every conceivable means of transportation raced full tilt over the potholed obstacle course. Vehicles went every which-way, communicating by a cacophonous beeping of horns. I began to understand what the phrase *a wing and a prayer* meant.

I felt like we were inside a pinball machine. All you could hear from us were gasps and stifled cries. We shared the streets with cars, buses, trucks, and carts drawn by horses and donkeys. Hundreds of motorbikes wove in and out between stalled traffic. Bicycles with multiple riders wobbled past pedestrians and men pushing carts. Groups of black veiled women, like flocks of ravens, gathered on corners. Any contraption that might move and carry people at the same time jockeyed for position. Vehicles, cutting across four lanes, sped on and off of the perilous traffic circles.

Everything imaginable was happening all at once, but in the apparent chaos all seemed to be working smoothly. It was one big dance. I was seeing a giant display of group mind. We all moved like a flock of birds or a school of fish, going where we needed to go, aware of each other and missing collision by fractions of an inch.

I relaxed a bit and took a tentative look above street level. The buildings were crammed together in every configuration and in all states of disrepair. Cairo is a city so old and so crowded that the only place to build is up. People live in tents on rooftops, and when they can afford it they build additional levels on top of the existing one. Structurally unsound and unable to bear the weight, many buildings collapse, taking the lives of the families within.

The endless trappings of a grossly overcrowded city cluttered the landscape. Clothes hung from lines strung across alleyways. Fruit and vegetable stands vied with merchandise spilling out of storefronts, tempting passersby. Rejected furniture and household items were piled on crumbling curbs. And again, people were everywhere.

Craning our necks out the windows, we oohed and aahed. We bounced from one side of the van to the other, not wanting to miss any of the sights. Finally we stopped in front of the Hotel Victoria, an old brick building in a nondescript downtown neighborhood.

It was already after noon when we checked in and took the ancient elevator to our rooms. Khalidah and I were assigned to be roommates. We walked down the long narrow, dimly lit hallway and opened the tall door with a heavy old black metal key. Choosing a bed, I immediately dropped onto the overstuffed mattress and was out like a light.

I fell into a deep sleep and awoke to a sound both strange and familiar. Struggling out of bed, I opened the shuttered windows to let in the glorious voices of the muezzins chanting the mid-afternoon *call to prayer* from the towering minarets.

I thought I was in heaven; the sound of angels echoed back and forth in rounds. The whole city was vibrating with a spiritual, otherworldly quality. On the street below, men came from their shops and rolled out their prayer rugs on the sidewalk. Amidst the hubbub of traffic and activity, they prostrated themselves, making their prayers facing Mecca.

Later I ate dinner alone in the hotel dining room. Most of the group had raced off to get a head start on seeing the local dancers, but I wanted to rest and prepare for our excursion to the pyramids the next day.

In the morning we boarded a minibus to take us to the pyramids. I was relieved to be traveling in such a small group. My excitement grew as we approached the three massive structures. I was surprised to see them so close to the city and felt again that they weren't as I recalled them. I remembered them as being isolated, a long ride through the desert. Now, the sprawl of the city came right up to the site. Rounding a bend, they were directly in front of us.

The entrance road was lined with shops overflowing with souvenirs. A long line of buses wound up the curved pavement to the parking lot. Ejecting their passengers, they parked opposite the line of camels waiting to take tourists into the desert. Endless tables of tchotckes glittered in the sun. Miniature pyramids, scarabs, and sphinxes jumbled together in a variety of sizes and materials making none of them appealing. This was definitely not the way I had imagined or remembered things from my past life. Saddened and annoyed, I looked around expecting to see a McDonalds.

Khalidah, Debbie, Tom and I were the first out of the bus. As we walked together from the parking lot across the sandy plateau of Giza, I remembered what Prema had told me about the true purpose of the Great Pyramid of Cheops. "Though there is a sarcophagus, they never found anyone buried inside. Yes," she had said, "some other pyramids were the final resting place of the pharaohs after their death. But the Great Pyramid had a different use.

"Members of the true mystical traditions, both past and present, knew the Great Pyramid as a temple of initiation. As students of the Mystery Schools, they underwent long and intensive study and rituals to purify and balance their physical, emotional, and spiritual energies. Then, after years of training and many tests, the initiates were escorted deep within the pyramid to the King's Chamber for their final initiation.

"There in that small square room, the initiate was placed in the great granite sarcophagus and left alone in the absolute darkness. A massive cosmic energy penetrated the original capstone of the pyramid, focusing a fiery light ray directly into the King's Chamber. Built for this purpose, the dimensions and placement of the pyramid created a vibration that changed the molecular makeup of the body and allowed the initiate to handle a higher energy. This potent force would cause injury or death to the unbalanced or unrefined body and ravage the impure mind. Those who came out of the experience with their minds and bodies intact became vehicles for this higher energy and were a blessing to all." Prema was part of the lineage extending back to these Mystery Schools, and my studies with her were preparing me for a similar destiny. I hoped to experience the transformative power of the King's Chamber.

Our guide handed us our tickets to enter the Great Pyramid. Climbing through the grand foyer up to the King's Chamber tested my resolve. Already disillusioned by the crowds of people, I ducked, then crouched, then bent double to avoid hitting my head as I moved further into the interior. I began to feel the pressure of all the stone bearing down on me. Not usually claustrophobic, I started hyperventilating.

I entered the King's Chamber and stood squashed up against the wall. People jabbered and joked all around us. I'd come so far and now with all the inane comments, we could have been in a shopping mall. The chattering tourists weren't cooperating with my desire for a deep spiritual experience.

Slowly people began to filter out of the chamber, and I was left alone with my traveling companions. I stood quietly waiting for the next onslaught of tourists, but none came. Then brazenly, I went to the sarcophagus, climbed in and lay down. It felt familiar, like I'd been there before. Then I gasped as a wave of horror from some long forgotten experience washed over me. It wasn't a vision but a physical sensation so frightening that I sat bolt upright. I quickly climbed out, terrified that my arrogance would be punished.

I leaned up against the wall then slowly slipped down the smooth stones, coming to rest on the floor. The hard rock on my bottom grounded me. Closing my eyes, I felt the walls begin to pulsate. I could hear a faint sound of voices that turned into a chant which grew louder and louder. The sound became a deafening roar, and the heaviness of the millions of tons of stone above me created an unbearable pressure. I felt an energy running up and down my spine. The thunderous sound literally rattled my bones, turning my backbone into a tuning fork. The dissonant chord built to a crescendo then the top of my head felt like it exploded, unleashing a blinding light…

My eyes flash open. The stone walls are transparent. I'm sitting in a pyramid of crystal white light. I experience myself as pure energy. I've been here forever and will continue on into eternity. I see the desert before the pyramid was even conceived, then I watch the structure rising from the sand as thousands of builders labor over its creation. I observe the rituals of other awakening initiates, and the terror, and then the freedom of those who go beyond their rational minds. I see the centuries when the pyramid disappeared, covered first by the floodwaters and later by sand. I sense the excitement of those who see it again for the first time. I witness an endless stream of visitors making their way through this chamber. The string of visions unfolds for eons. I am the consciousness of the pyramid itself, experiencing its history.

Slowly, I once again became conscious of Khalidah, Debbie, Tom, and I, still alone in the King's chamber. I could see from the expressions in their wide-open eyes that they too had experienced something astonishing. In that moment I knew that we were destined to come and sit opposite each other within these four walls. Together we created a certain chord, a sound that fixed the pattern of our experience. Hearing others approach, we rose in unison and crawled silently out of the pyramid.

Back on the bus, our tour group was taken to a restaurant where the four of us sat quietly together. At first we were each lost in our own world. Eventually we began speaking at once. "What happened? What did you see? What did it mean?" We questioned each other excitedly. The content of our experiences wasn't exactly the same, but we'd each encountered a transcendent all-consuming light.

When we settled down a bit, we talked about our lives and what had led us to Egypt. Recounting our stories, we found we shared a lifelong fascination with this land and a lifelong obsession with death. All of us had been confronted at young tender ages with the mysteries of death.

Khalidah's mother was murdered when she was eleven years old. Debbie's brother committed suicide when she was twelve. Tom actually lived his whole childhood in the Texas funeral home that was his family's business. His chores from a very young age included sweeping the room where the deceased were embalmed.

After a string of sudden deaths in my own family, my father, though physically healthy and relatively young, fell victim to a paralyzing fear of his own impending demise. His condition overshadowed my whole childhood; death became our family's constant companion. I, too, became obsessed with this stalker, who did indeed finally claim my father when I was thirteen. Thinking I was next, I studied death as if I might somehow learn to elude it.

Gathered around the table in that crowded restaurant, we each shared our feelings of kinship with this land permeated by the remnants of its ancestors' preoccupation with death. Immersed in the idea of immortality, the ancient religion and rituals revolved around preparing to live through eternity in a glorious afterworld. Our individual experiences in the pyramid confirmed for each of us that we were following trails that reached beyond our present existence.

The next several days were a round of typical tourist activities, though each experience was exciting and fresh for me. During the day our group visited all the usual sites—the mosques, the Egyptian Museum with the King Tut exhibit, and the oldest step pyramid at Saqqara. At the papyrus factory, we watched as reeds from the river were turned into sheets of paper and painted with reproductions of the tomb walls. Everyone looked forward, though, to the ultimate *shop until you drop* experience.

The ancient shopping bazaar at Khan El Khalili did not disappoint. Entering the souk from a relatively modern street, we turned the corner into a world apart. The road narrowed to a shadowed maze of shops and open-air stalls. Spices, copper trays, jewelry, pottery, leather goods, and finely embroidered clothing all bunched together to create an overwhelming abundance of exotic merchandise and dizzying sensory stimulation.

Turning into an even smaller alleyway, we threaded our way between an old striped barbershop pole and a glass shop with hundreds of delicate handblown perfume bottles in its window. Making a few twists and turns, we passed through a doorway and up a flight of stairs to the end of the second floor. We found ourselves in a shop filled from floor to ceiling with bellydance costumes and supplies. Folded black fabric hip scarves lined one whole side of the room. This arrangement was repeated on the next wall in red fabric, then the next was turquoise, and the fourth wall was royal blue. All were triangular or rectangular hip wraps decorated with finely crocheted beaded or coined borders. In the next room, the floor was carpeted with sequined bras and belts, while the walls were hung with skirts, veils, and beledi dresses in a myriad of colors and fabrics. My companions began tearing through the stacks like kids on Christmas morning.

I chatted and negotiated with Mahmoud, the proprietor of this bellydancer heaven, about having costumes made for my troupe. Then I selected hip scarves and veils to sell to my students and indulged in an extravagant black sequined bra and belt with multicolored appliqués for me. By that time, I was on overload. The other women, more practiced at retail therapy, were unfazed and just getting their second wind.

Needing to clear my head, I ventured alone into the souk. Normally I have an unfailing sense of direction. Trying to stay conscious of the twists and turns I took through the narrow alleyways, I promptly got lost. I must have gone in one door of a store and out another that opened onto an entirely different street. I tried to find my way back to Mahmoud's shop, but I wandered around getting more and more lost. Nothing looked familiar.

Panicking, I sat down at a table at a sidewalk cafe. The sights and sounds, and particularly the smells, were overwhelming me. The energy drained from my body, and I felt like I was going to faint.

Suddenly I was seeing myself from afar. My consciousness hovered above me and the miasma of activity. From beyond the rooftops, I saw myself sitting below, and at the same time I could see Mahmoud's shop several blocks away. I recognized it by the striped barbershop pole and the perfume bottles in the window next to it. Then just as quickly, I was again inside my body. Making my way back through the labyrinth, I slipped thankfully into Mahmoud's shop.

I was contemplating this bewildering out-of-body experience when two old women, dressed in black with headscarves tightly covering their hair, came through the door. They opened their dirty tote bags and out spilled the most sparkling elegant costumes.

Sipping the tea Mahmoud's young assistant had offered them, they sat along the bench opposite me as he inspected their work. We observed each other from across the room. Perhaps they wondered about the life I led—one that allowed a young woman like me to dance in public in immodest costumes like the ones that they created.

I, on the other hand, was learning a great lesson about presumption. These were women I would have passed on the street without notice, or maybe with a feeling of pity on seeing the soiled sacks they lugged around. While actually they were the artists creating the incredible treasures I'd traveled halfway around the globe to purchase.

Finished with his inspection, Mahmoud handed them folded money that they tucked inside their bosoms. They rose, nodded to me, and as they departed, the older woman fixed me with a piercing gaze as if to affirm my insight. I purchased a vibrant striped and beaded hip scarf that she had made. I needed it to remember this sobering lesson—*stay awake, Sherry. Things are not always, nor even often, as they seem.*

At sundown we bussed back to our hotel, napped until ten o'clock, then dressed to go out. This was to be our nightly modus operandi. With jet lag and Cairo time, in a city where the nightlife didn't begin until midnight, we slept through the early evening then walked bleary-eyed to our van. Staying up into the wee hours of the morning, we watched the performances of all the most famous dancers.

Nagua Fuad and her large cast of dancers and musicians were electrifying. With passion and panache she fulfilled her reputation as Cairo's long reigning dance queen. Up there in years, she was still more glamorous than all the supporting dancers who were half her age. Her elegant posture inspired me, and her engaging personality delighted me. Using an extensive vocabulary of steps, she interpreted each instrument and brilliantly illustrated every nuance of the musical compositions. It looked like the sound was pouring directly from her body.

We waited for Soheir Zaki to appear at her own nightclub, a floating houseboat on the Nile. She finally made her entrance after one a.m. Known as the Sweetheart of Cairo, she also was a mature woman with a long illustrious career behind her.

As she danced, the audience of mostly Saudi men sang along with her band. They waved their arms above their heads while shouting exclamations. Then with stacks of currency in hand, they crossed the floor to shower Soheir with fistfuls of Egyptian pounds. Converting the pounds into U.S. currency, I counted at least two thousand dollars on the floor—and by local time it was still early evening.

That was the heyday of Egyptian tourism. People from all over the Middle East came to party in Cairo where, unlike the more strict Moslem Gulf countries, there were no laws against serving liquor. Every night superstar singers and famous bellydancers packed the nightclubs in lavish five-star hotels. Musicians, and dancers with flaming candelabras balanced on their heads, led guests through sumptuous hotel lobbies to wedding receptions and other festivities.

The men were dark and handsome, and the women were glamorous and chic in their designer dresses. The air—rich with the scent of Chanel No.5, Shalimar, and other sophisticated fragrances—exuded an atmosphere of wealth and luxury.

I saw romance as I never had before. Men were men and women, women. Sexuality hung in the air. The women used their eyes for maximum effect—a glance spoke volumes and promised more. While we in the West turn our heads to look directly at others, these dark-eyed beauties merely glanced from the corners of their eyes, creating a mysterious, coy and provocative allure. Young, upfront, in-your-face American women, who have lost the fine art of flirting, could learn a lot from these women.

The new up-and-coming dancers impressed us. Lucy held court at the Sheraton Hotel on a huge stage, her technique obviously influenced by ballet and jazz. But to me, she just couldn't compare with either Nagua or Soheir in the feelings she evoked or in her ability to engage her audience.

Dina, in four-inch heels with a thirty-five-piece orchestra behind her, created a sensation. I took photos of her controversial new costumes—miniscule dresses barely covering her tightly controlled shimmies. Her hot pants with sheer pantaloons caused a lot of raised eyebrows and whispered comments among both men and women. She definitely captured everyone's attention.

Dina's expressions alternated between ecstatic and flirtatious. Everyone loved her *joie de vivre* as she included everyone in her fun. Of all the rising stars, she was the most creative, developing her own innovative style. Unlike the others, her movements were small and contained. She dove deep inside the music, drawing us into her passion and joy.

I excitedly awaited Fifi Abdo. I'd seen a video of her floating down from the ceiling on a platform, alighting on the stage like a fairy princess. That night she came flying out of the left wing, leapt into a split, rose gracefully and circled the stage to greet her adoring audience. Her beauty, her voluptuous body clothed in the most magnificent of costumes, and her wildly abandoned shimmies were all that I had hoped for.

The two folkloric performances we saw gave us a rich education in the history of Egyptian dance. One show was at a hotel and the other at the Balloon Theater with the highly acclaimed Reda Troupe of Egypt. Mahmoud Reda, the director of the company, had traveled across Egypt studying and collecting the dances from each region and village and then adapting them for the stage. He single-handedly revived and preserved dances that were on the brink of extinction. We saw dances influenced by desert life and those by fishermen casting their nets. We watched the *hagallah* wedding dance and other social dances all presented in a fabulous array of native costumes. The dances echoed the long rich and varied culture of the Egyptian people, while the powerful drum rhythms awakened the gods whose spirits filled the theater. All this was mesmerizing, yet I excitedly awaited our departure for Luxor which, I felt sure, held the ancient Egypt of my memories.

CHAPTER 16:
TEMPLES AND TOMBS

Midmorning our plane landed in Luxor—Thebes of antiquity. Loaded onto a bus, we bounced over country roads lined with date palms framing oxen-plowed fields. In my heart I knew I had come home. Without a doubt I had lived here before. The skyline, the landscape, the smells, even the feel of the air on my skin was familiar. As the Nile came into view, I gazed across to the Valley of the Kings on the opposite bank, remembering it as clearly as I did my own front yard at home.

Turning onto the cobblestone road bordering the banks of the Nile, we saw the ruins of the great temple of Karnak spread out before us. A couple of miles further south, the smaller Luxor Temple appeared. Flashes of myself walking this sacred land pierced the present landscape. My posture straightened as I felt the significance of the rituals that took place in these two temples. I remembered walking down the majestic sphinx lined road connecting them.

The bus came to a halt as we reached our hotel, the old but still elegant Winter Palace, with its line of horse drawn carriages waiting in front. After checking in, Khalidah and I raced out to explore. Walking in rhythm with each other, our shoes clicked over the cobblestones. Excited to be in Luxor, we meandered down the boulevard then were drawn back into the shaded streets to the rear of the hotel. Modest shops were interspersed with tightly packed dwellings. Some of the homes were hidden behind mud walls while others fronted on the street. We glanced discreetly inside the open doors and windows, curious to see how the local people lived.

Tantalizing aromas escaped from within. Mouths watering, we realized we were ravenous. We hadn't eaten breakfast and it was well past lunchtime. Stopping in at a small restaurant with scuffed linoleum floors and grey formica-topped tables, we ordered *kushari*—the local dish made from pasta, lentils, rice, and onions. It was delicious. We lingered awhile longer sipping *karkady*—a tart, bright red tea steeped from hibiscus flowers. We left calling out, "Shukran, thank you," one of the few Arabic words we knew.

We found ourselves on the road leading to the Luxor Temple. The feeling of familiarity was so strong that I was sure I'd been there before. I also felt that Khalidah and I had walked these pathways together many centuries before. Approaching the temple, my mind's eye saw it as it had originally appeared. Two seated granite statues of Ramses II framed the ceremonial entrance along with two monumental obelisks. Four more standing Ramses fronted the massive pylon. I didn't know whether I was remembering a rendering of the reconstructed temple or the real thing.

Coming to a shady spot, we sat down on the crumbling remains of a carved stone wall at the base of a standing column. Khalidah began to speak. Echoing my unvoiced feeling of familiarity, she said with complete conviction, "I remember when we first came to the temple." Her large brown eyes, beautiful black skin, and regal carriage spoke of the possibility of a local heritage even in this lifetime. She looked like an oracle as she told the story of our shared ancient past.

Khalidah described two young girls. Frightened and missing our families, we had arrived on a felluca from a village up the Nile to prepare for our lives as temple priestesses. As she further retraced the events of that life, I recognized details of my vision of the Opet Festival. She was describing the same day I had relived in Prema's garden. When I asked if she'd ever heard of that particular festival, she shook her head, "Never before. The words just popped out of my mouth, but I saw it clear as day."

We sat silently contemplating the seeming coincidence. Then we enthusiastically exchanged stories about our present lives. The more we talked, the more we saw that our experiences mirrored each other. We both taught bellydance in our own schools. We each had a large performing troupe, and we were both dedicated to the mystical and spiritual elements of the dance. We freely shared our teaching experiences, she in Chicago and I in California. From the vast possibilities of Middle Eastern music and dance styles, our repertoires of performance pieces included remarkably similar material. No other teachers we'd met thus far had the same orientation as we did.

Talking into the late afternoon, we traded notes about how we used the dance as a vehicle for expressing deep truths. We felt with certainty that we'd originally learned these spiritual principles together in the temple here at Luxor. It was a joy for me to find such a kindred soul.

Early the next morning our group boarded the ferry that took us across the Nile to the Valley of the Kings. The sun rose behind us, beginning its path across the sky to eventually set beyond the western bank. The ancient Egyptians called this side of the Nile the Land of the Dead. I recalled the legend of Ra, the sun god. Every morning he launched his ship from the eastern horizon, sailed across the heavens, then disappeared each evening into the underworld.

When our ferry reached the shore we were greeted by the Colossi of Mennon, two, fifty-feet tall, seated statues of Pharaoh Amenophis III. Busing through the small village, we arrived at the Valley of the Kings where we spent hours wandering in and out of the network of tombs hidden beneath the sandy hills. We descended from the barren neutral-colored desertscape into underground rooms where walls and ceilings were painted in still brilliant colors. The sight of them was startling and breathtaking. Here were the very paintings I'd spent hours pouring over in books since the second grade, when I'd chosen Egypt for my first geography report. I'd been imagining this moment for years, and I wasn't disappointed.

One particular tomb seemed familiar to both Khalidah and me. I felt like I knew every detail of the paintings surrounding me. Though I couldn't read them, I sensed that the hieroglyphics described circumstances and events that I had actually lived through. Even the people depicted looked recognizable to me. The longer I studied them, the more I had the eerie feeling that we were two of the temple dancers portrayed on the mural. Had she and I lain here with the pharaoh, waiting to be transported to the afterlife?

Rather than take the ferry with the rest of the group, Khalidah and I hired a felucca to take us back across the Nile. As we drifted away from the Land of the Dead, I felt myself shifting back and forth between my present day tourist self and the priestess self of my far distant past. When we reached the other shore, instead of crossing the street to the hotel, I inadvertently turned in the direction of the Luxor Temple, thinking I was on my way home.

That evening a private party was arranged for our group in an intimate restaurant on one of the back streets of Luxor. We boarded horse-drawn carriages at sunset and trotted off through the narrow roads. Passing by the modest houses, we again peeked through open doors and windows, hoping to catch a glimpse of family life.

At the restaurant two very handsome and gracious waiters served us tea and *mezze*—tasty appetizers. We dipped our *aish baladi*—bread made from whole-wheat flour—into a variety of chickpea, eggplant, and sesame seed pastes. Tightly woven tapestries and intricately patterned rugs covered every inch of the walls and floor, creating the quintessential atmosphere for our arriving entertainers.

Three musicians greeted us, saying, *"Assalamu Alaikum,"* peace be unto you. Sitting on low cushions, they began playing the traditional instruments their ancestors had used for thousands of years. One man pulled a bow across the string of his rababa while another set a dynamic and compelling rhythm with his dumbec. The third man blew into his *mizmar*, a small trumpet shaped metal instrument with a high-pitched sound used to charm snakes.

While the ancient sensuous music filled the small space, whiffs of simmering spices drifted in from the kitchen. Suddenly two women burst into the room, their finger cymbals loudly tapping out *tekka dum, tekka dum*. They were costumed in full-length dresses completely covered with long strands of beaded fringe which shook, trembled, swayed, and whipped around their powerful hip twists and thrusts. The energy they created in that room with just three musicians and two dancers could have filled a rock concert stadium.

As the waiters cleared our dinner plates from the table, the dancers pulled us up to join them. Urging us on, they played their cymbals next to our hips and showed us how to move. What a thrill! Khairiyyah and Reja, two of the four sisters of the Maazin family, traced their lineage back to the gypsies of India who migrated to Egypt. They called themselves Ghawazee, which means invaders of the heart. Renowned throughout the entire region, they and their other two sisters had entertained at celebrations for years.

The family was beloved by the local people, but dancing wasn't appropriate work for a married woman in Egypt. As single women they danced to earn money for their dowry then stopped when they wed. When we saw them, only the two sisters were still performing. Though I'm not usually star struck, dancing with these women who were so much a part of the folklore of bellydance history was a fairytale come true. We danced till we dropped then, like Cinderella we climbed back into our carriages and returned to our Winter Palace.

CHAPTER 17: RITUALS, REMEMBRANCE, AND REBIRTH

T he next evening I stood in front of the Winter Palace waiting for someone to come for me. I'd spent the day meditating alone at Karnak then searching through the surrounding area for the small jewelry shop that Prema had told me about. She said that if I found the shop, and if the proprietor felt the timing was right, he would contact some local dervishes. If they agreed, I might be allowed to join their zikr.

I'd found the shopkeeper, but he didn't give me a definitive answer. Instead he told me to wait by the entrance to my hotel. So I was very relieved when a man in a brown and white striped *galibeya* approached me and whispered, "Zikr?" I followed him across the street where we boarded a felucca to cross the Nile. It was Thursday night, the beginning of the Muslim holy day when Sufis perform the ritual zikr, which means remembrance.

The sun was setting as we reached the opposite shore. We walked quickly down a dirt road and approached a small dwelling set amidst an enclave of other homes. My companion left me at an open doorway, indicating that I was to watch from there. I was disappointed but realized that in Muslim countries women weren't allowed to worship with the men.

Peering around the doorpost, I saw fifteen men lining the room, sitting with their backs against the walls. Soon they were chanting, "*La illah ha illallah,*" there is no God but God, while rolling their heads from side to side. At home I'd taken part in a few zikrs with people who had adopted and embraced Sufism as a spiritual practice. The men in this room had been raised in the Muslim faith. Here in Egypt I felt once again that I was dipping into the source.

I tried to remember not to get lost in the glamour of things. Prema had told me that the ritual was no more real or authentic just because people are born into the Way. "It is the intention and commitment of the individual person that makes a rite sacred, not the act itself." Yet I could feel this room was permeated with intention and was rich with commitment. With this many people reverently invoking the one God, I quickly fell into an ecstatic trance. As this most sacred chant affirmed, I experienced that all is one and all is God.

At the end of the evening as I was leaving, I asked one of the women if it would be possible for me to attend a *Zar* ceremony. From the moment Prema had first mentioned this particular ritual, I was intrigued and wanted to know more about it. She had said that the Zar ceremony is almost always conducted for women, and that it can be thought of as an ancient form of group therapy or an exorcism of sorts. With roots in the countries south of Egypt, probably originating in Ethiopia, the practice had spread through many North African countries and into Saudi Arabia.

Prema had explained that Zar practitioners believed depression, infertility, and other assorted physical and psychological disorders were caused by evil spirits. When a woman had an illness or affliction caused by these demons, she and her female friends and family came together to hold a ceremony. Through drumming, dancing, and offerings of gifts and food, the community would pacify these hostile spirits and cleanse the afflicted woman.

Prema had further mentioned that these gatherings were also a way for women—suppressed in their male dominated cultures—to meet, share, and let off steam in ways usually considered inappropriate for 'good' women. Fascinated by these unusual practices, I'd make a comment that maybe a Zar ceremony could help me.

Now as I followed one of my hosts through the house, I was hopeful that I'd be able to actually witness a Zar ceremony. Leading me into the kitchen, she spoke softly to several of the other women. They talked rapidly in Arabic, shaking their heads "yes" and "no" while observing me with their dark, penetrating eyes. Finally she turned and told me that one of the women had a sister who lived across the river. She had recently had one Zar but needed another. Unfortunately she didn't have the money necessary to pay the musicians. If I would be willing to pay, they would see if something could be arranged for the following night.

It was great good luck and perfect timing as we had just one more evening left in Luxor. Saying they would come for me if it could be arranged, they refused the money I offered them. "You wouldn't have been allowed to come to zikr if you weren't to be trusted. If we come for you, give us money then."

The next evening I again waited outside the entrance of the Winter Palace. It was getting late, and I was just about to give up when a woman approached and said, "*Yalla*, come." She led me through the back streets to the south of town. My explorations of Luxor hadn't taken me in that direction. I would have liked to invite Khalidah along, but Prema had insisted I seek out and attend these rituals on my own. She explained that it was important to know if my energy and intention, alone, would be sufficient to open the door to these usually private rituals. She also suggested that I experience them on my own, so I wouldn't be distracted in any way.

Finally arriving at a walled dwelling, we entered the gate. We walked through an empty courtyard and then into the dimly lit house. Hearing voices, we turned in their direction. A number of women of all ages sat or stood talking in the modestly furnished living room. There was a friendly, comfortable feeling. They eyed me curiously, nodding and smiling.

When the musicians came, the woman I'd spoken with the previous night approached me, rubbing her fingers together in the universal sign for money. I didn't know how much it would be, but I handed her a bunch of Egyptian pounds that she quickly counted. Satisfied, she took the money to the female musicians.

As the drummers warmed up, a middle-aged woman wearing a wrinkled white caftan was led into the room. Looking distressed and disoriented, she sat down on the floor with her back against the wall. I recognized the woman who was helping her from the night before.

The musicians circled the room playing tambourines and frame drums while the other women began dancing to the hypnotic rhythm. Making little shuffling *step-slide-steps* counterclockwise around the room, they threw their arms up and down in beckoning and gathering gestures as if invoking spirits from above. They tossed their heads from side to side, trying to fling the demons from their hair.

As the musicians switched rhythms, a few women moved to the center of the floor, undulating to the music in a slinky and suggestive way. Each time the cadence changed, others came forward and danced with their own distinctly unique movements, which reflected the character of the drumbeat. Some appeared angular and disjointed while others wafted airily around the room. I was familiar with several of the rhythms, but others I'd never heard before. They varied from short broken beats that made me feel nervous, to longer livelier patterns that brought out my joyous side.

The woman in white remained huddled on the floor with a glazed look in her eyes. Suddenly as the rhythm switched again, she was on her feet dancing as if possessed. She looked like a completely different person. Her body shook and jerked about erratically. Her breath was heavy and she uttered strange, grunting sounds and anguished cries. The other women hovered around her, leading her back to the open area when she got too close to the furnishings. While giving her space to move freely, they kept her from falling and hurting herself.

As the music got faster and faster, she kept pace with it. Women around her clapped and made the zagareet sound, the piercing trills of their ululations urging her on. She danced frantically, trying to loosen the grip of whatever had a hold on her. The energy got more and more intense, the air thick with unleashed emotion.

Finally the frenzied woman collapsed in a heap and was carried to the side of the room where she was propped up against the wall. The musicians stopped playing, packed their instruments and silently left. Steaming pots of tea and trays of sweets were brought from the kitchen.

I was shocked at how suddenly it was over. It sure beat spending years on a shrink's couch rehashing the same old problems. I remember thinking, *Let's just get down and shake that nasty little spirit right out of our hair.* I'd personally experienced the power of music and dance to heal. There, in a tradition that had survived for centuries and was fully supported by the community, the potential would be magnified. The women had come together and set a unified intention. Then invoking their spirit allies, they danced in full belief that the spell would be broken and their friend would be restored to health.

Looking around the room, everything seemed normal, like just another tea party. Some of the women ate and socialized while others attended to the exhausted woman, wiping her forehead with wet towels and smoothing her hair. I was struck by the serene look on her flushed face as she smiled lovingly at her companions. I still wasn't quite sure I understood what I'd seen, or if it was really valuable in the long run. But her sister approached me and taking my hand, said over and over, "Shukran, shukran, thank you."

I spent the last morning of our stay at the Luxor Temple. Alone this time, I hurried through the ruins searching for the place of my Opet Festival vision, the one I'd had the day I sat beading in Prema's garden. I felt sure that it had to be in this temple, but so little of the structure was still standing and nothing looked familiar.

The place was deserted, the hoards of tourists still lingering over their leisurely breakfasts. I stopped and asked my intuition for guidance then waited quietly, listening and looking for direction. Expecting a thought or words or a visual sign of some kind, I stood attentively. The air was perfectly still, not a hint of a breeze. There was absolute silence, nothing moved. Disappointed, I relaxed for a moment and was just about to give up when I felt a strong push from behind that set me in motion. My shadow, long with the morning sun at my back, led the way. *Zaye el hawa...like the wind* I thought as I flew down corridors of rubble, past rows of broken columns.

Out of breath, I stopped. Though early in the day, the sun beat down on my uncovered head. Dizzy from the heat, I had to sit. Beads of sweat rolled down my forehead and into my eyes, and as I wiped them away the column in front of me came sharply into focus. Faded hieroglyphics jumped out at me. They were the very same ones from my vision that long ago day in Prema's garden. I was astonished on the one hand, but on the other, discovering the glyphs exactly as I'd seen them seemed inevitable. Part of me had felt certain that I would find a sign confirming my vision, but another part of me was still continually amazed by these incidents that showed me that life is so much grander and more miraculous than I'd ever imagined.

I studied the column more closely. Again I knew what the symbols meant, but this time neither the words nor the vision faded. In stone, right before my eyes, the message was loud and clear: 'Know thyself, and thou shalt know the Universe and God.'

A feeling of peace rained down like a blessing on me. I felt re-born. I'd begun my journey wrapped in old ideas and images. But like my five-year-old self in my recurring nightmare, I didn't want to be a mummy, carefully preserved and waiting for a glorious afterlife. I wanted to live fully in this lifetime.

Looking back over my journey, I saw how blessed I was to find Prema. With her wisdom and intuition she had guided me through lessons that peeled away my false self, revealing who I truly am. From her I'd learned to stay awake and to use all of my experiences as mirrors that reflect life as it really is, not as I'd been led to believe it was. The discipline of the Temple Dance allowed me to focus, come into the present moment, and know without doubt where I must always begin.

The bellydance had ushered me onto the path of Beauty and had taught me to love myself and know that I held true radiance within. As a performer I learned to express this inner knowing and share this grace, this baraka, as a healing gift. I, too, became a doorway through which Beauty could enter the world.

Prema, Narendra, Gabie, and Alan had all told me, in their different ways, that I must come to know myself completely. Sitting amidst the ruins, looking at the ancient and timeless hieroglyphics, confirmed that I'd indeed come full circle. I'd been guided back to my beginning.

Lost in the desert of a life without vision, I'd been led into this oasis of dance. The dance had invaded my heart, casting out my doubts and fears, leaving room only for love. The veil had finally lifted, and my way was clearly evident and undeniably affirmed. I'd found my life's work. I'd been entrusted to impart the secrets hidden behind the veil to students of my own. With renewed conviction I gladly committed myself to a life of service.

Looking around me at the remains of this magnificent temple, I felt grateful beyond expression. Here in Egypt I'd returned to the Source. I'd been called home to be reminded of who I was long before being born into this lifetime. Finally I knew myself and my proper place in the Universe. Now I was ready to return home to my life in California. The door to my true path had once again opened and this time, without hesitation, I rose and stepped through.

I flew home ready and inspired to resume my teaching. My time in Egypt, though far too short, revealed to me my place in a long and sacred lineage. With my own eyes I'd seen the actual sites of my visions. The words on the column in the Luxor Temple were engraved on my soul. If I lost my way again they would remind me of my direction. My initiation in the Great Pyramid completed the link in the chain that bound me to my destiny.

As soon as I arrived, I made the trip down the coast to see Prema. Meeting me at the door with Krishna at her feet and keys in hand, she looked happy to see me. Taking a short drive to Meditation Mount, we sat gazing out over the valley. Full of my newfound certainty, I told Prema the details of my journey. Knowing no words would suffice, I thanked her for initiating me into the ways of a temple priestess and for guiding me on my difficult journey. I finished by confiding how relaxing it was to have finally reached the end of my search.

Prema listened and nodded patiently then asked if I'd be willing to take one more inner journey. Out of respect I agreed. "Close your eyes," she said. "Travel back to Egypt to the Great Pyramid." I was happy to do so, and instantly I saw the plateau at Giza.

"Where are you?" I heard Prema asking me. "Find yourself on the Pyramid…"

Immediately I glance up to the top of the Great Pyramid, but I don't see myself. I drop my gaze a bit further, but again I can't find myself. My eyes travel lower and lower toward the base of the pyramid and still, I'm not there. Finally I see myself standing amidst the scattered debris on the very first step. So tiny, barely visible, I'm holding on for dear life as I gaze up at the dizzying height. Searching for a way up to the next step, it suddenly dawns on me what this means.

I realize that my work thus far is just the initial step in my eternal journey…I have this pyramid to climb and beyond it are other heights to scale. This is only my first initiation into the life of a priestess. Wonder and humility at the immense grandeur of life sweeps over me. Although I am teaching now, I know that I will always be a student. I understand that I'm fortunate to have come even this far, and I'm filled with gratitude. As I surrender to the long road ahead, a flicker of light appears above me. Gathering my energy into my center, I affirm my intention and pull myself up to stand before an opening doorway. Without a second thought, I joyfully cross the threshold.

EPILOGUE

I stand in the center of my dance studio waiting for my student to arrive. She enters and takes her place behind me. Gazing at her in the mirror, I know we have stood this way a thousand times before. Although we don't appear as we did in the past, the eyes that watch each other haven't changed. In different lands and in different temples, we have come together again and again to travel into the heart of the moment. Now she waits expectantly for me to begin. I raise my arms and the stillness of the ages descends. The present time falls away and we stand, priestess and aspiring student, waiting at the doorway to ecstasy.

The End

ACKNOWLEDGEMENTS

Deepest gratitude goes to:

Lori Felton, my editor and writing teacher. Guiding someone through any artistic process is a delicate balance of listening and suggesting, pushing and retreating, critiquing and encouraging the student to be bold and find her own voice. Lori answered, "I can't do that," with, "Why not?" She led me with exquisite sensitivity, making the writing process so exciting I couldn't wait to begin my next book. I am forever grateful and lucky that she is also my sister.

Prema Devi opened the door and taught me to see my dance training as a spiritual practice. She knew how to deal with my impatience and desire to learn everything at once. I saw many students come and go, not recognizing this once in a lifetime opportunity to learn so much more than Bellydance. With her tough love, she gave me the gift of beginner's mind.

Reshad Field, mystic, spiritual teacher, and author of *The Last Barrier, To Know We're Loved,* and *Alchemy of the Heart* among many other spiritual classics. Through his Living School, he teaches with great wisdom, originality, humor, and the magic to reach really hard cases like me.

Bob Rasmussen, world-renowned master healer, saved my life more than once.

Adnan Sarhan, Sufi master and teacher of mystical dance and music, who shares his intelligence of the heart as he tirelessly travels the world.

Gabie Blackburn, Narendra Rathor, Allen and Helen Hooker—Ojai legends and loving souls who graced me with their wisdom and kindness.

My dance teachers extrordinaire:

Horacio Cifuentes, by his very presence he taught me elegance and refinement in the dance.

Bobby Farrah showed me how much more emotion I could

dare and bare on stage.

Bert Balladine encouraged me to slow down and be the cool blonde that I am, rather than try to be some hot tamale.

Shukriya invited me to be a *Dancer of the Pharoahs* and taught me how to beautifully present large groups of inexperienced dancers onstage.

My many teachers in Egypt, Turkey and Morocco who shared with me the very essence of their cultures.

My students and past and present members of Troupe Ala Nar, Rising Stars, Mystic East Dancers, Shimmy Amour,and ZIA. Teaching them is my spiritual practice. My intention in every class is to be present and allow the Spirit to move through me and inspire them to dance for the world.

Ruth Felton, my dear Mom, who raised three daughters almost single-handedly. She loved me and taught me just about everything I needed to know to venture out into the world with confidence. She continues to show me how to live a life of grace and humility.

Richard Brier, my love, traveling companion, hooky cohort, business partner, chef, walking thesaurus, proofreader, and holder of our shared history, both in this physical life and our many shared moments outside of time.

Lily Ecstasy Trueheart and LingLing Lovejoy, my beloved furry friends, for having hearts big enough for me to rest in.

ABOUT THE AUTHOR

Sherry Brier is director of Inner Rhythm Movement Arts Institute in Marin County, California. She spends her days dancing, teaching, choreographing dances for her students and two dance companies, writing, and playing hooky with her husband and cat. Frequent journeys to exotic lands and ancient cultures inspire her writing and choreographies.

Look for her upcoming book:
A DANCE OF YOUR OWN: Choreographing Your Life
(companion book to DOORWAY TO ECSTASY)

For information on
Classes, workshops, readings, events:
www.SherryBrier.com
www.InnerRhythmDance.com

Order books at:
Amazon.com
Your favorite local or online bookstore.

www.ingramcontent.com/pod-product-compliance
Lightning Source LLC
Chambersburg PA
CBHW052034090426
42739CB00010B/1906

* 9 7 8 0 9 8 9 8 4 6 3 0 1 *